"I wish I had this book when I began my writing journey. It's fresh, funny, thought-provoking, and provides important insights into the industry so that playwrights can get their work on stage immediately."
Antoinette Nwandu, *Award-Winning Playwright and Screenwriter,* Pass Over (Broadway), She's Gotta Have It (Netflix)

"I love this book! It is a clear-eyed, direct, practical guide for playwrights of all experience levels."
Allison Horsley, *Broadway Dramaturg and Translator,* Jersey Boys, The Cherry Orchard

"Goldfinger's workbook combines well curated examples with engaging exercises and evocative writing prompts to create an endless array of customizable approaches to playwriting. It speaks to the full range of those interested in creating scripted drama – students and teachers, novices and experts."
David S. Thompson, *Agnes Scott College*, Georgia

"A refreshing and galvanizing treatise on the craft of playwriting. Great for emerging playwrights!"
Yussef El Guindi, *Award-Winning Playwright,*
Back of th

"Read this book now. It is a gift to our students and our industry. It's going to revolutionize how we teach playwriting."

Jessica Bashline, *Director-Actor, Theater Professor at University of Miami*

"I'm going to put this book on the Required Reading list for acting and directing classes. Actors and directors need to know how plays function in order to do their best work."

Margaret Laurena Kemp, *Multi-Disciplinary Performance Artist, Theater Professor at University of California, Davis*

Playwriting with Purpose

Playwriting with Purpose: A Guide and Workbook for New Playwrights provides a holistic approach to playwriting from an award-winning playwright and instructor.

This book incorporates craft lessons by contemporary playwrights and provides concrete guidance for new and emerging playwrights. The author takes readers through the entire creative process, from creating characters and writing dialogue and silent moments to analyzing elements of well-made plays and creating an atmospheric environment. Each chapter is followed by writing prompts and pro tips that address unique facets of the conversation about the art and craft of playwriting. The book also includes information on the business of playwriting and a recommended reading list of published classic and contemporary plays, providing all the tools to successfully transform an idea into a script, and a script into a performance.

Playwriting with Purpose gives writers and students of playwriting hands-on lessons, artistic concepts, and business savvy to succeed in today's theater industry.

Jacqueline Goldfinger is an award-winning playwright, dramaturg, and librettist who seeks out unique collaborations, working across disciplines to create singular works of theater and opera. Her awards include the Yale Prize, the Opera America Discovery Grant, the Smith Prize, the Sloan Grant, the Independence Foundation Fellowship in the Arts, the Tennessee Williams Fellowship, and the Generations Award. She teaches workshops and seminars at college and university theater programs across the U.S., including at the University of California, Davis and San Diego, the University of Pennsylvania, and Temple University. For more information, visit www.jacquelinegoldfinger.com.

Playwriting with Purpose

A Guide and Workbook for New Playwrights

Jacqueline Goldfinger

NEW YORK AND LONDON

First published 2022
by Routledge
605 Third Avenue, New York, NY 10158

and by Routledge
2 Park Square, Milton Park, Abingdon, Oxon, OX14 4RN

Routledge is an imprint of the Taylor & Francis Group, an informa business

© 2022 Jacqueline Goldfinger

The right of Jacqueline Goldfinger to be identified as author of this work has been asserted by her in accordance with sections 77 and 78 of the Copyright, Designs and Patents Act 1988.

All rights reserved. No part of this book may be reprinted or reproduced or utilised in any form or by any electronic, mechanical, or other means, now known or hereafter invented, including photocopying and recording, or in any information storage or retrieval system, without permission in writing from the publishers.

Trademark notice: Product or corporate names may be trademarks or registered trademarks, and are used only for identification and explanation without intent to infringe.

Library of Congress Cataloging-in-Publication Data
Names: Goldfinger, Jacqueline, author.
Title: Playwriting with purpose : a guide and workbook for new
  playwrights / Jacqueline Goldfinger.
Description: New York, NY : Routledge, 2022. | Includes bibliographical
  references and index.
Identifiers: LCCN 2021007127 (print) | LCCN 2021007128
  (ebook) | ISBN 9781032003801 (hardback) | ISBN 9781032003818
  (paperback) | ISBN 9781003173885 (ebook)
Subjects: LCSH: Playwriting. | Drama—Technique.
Classification: LCC PN1661 .G64 2022 (print) | LCC PN1661
  (ebook) | DDC 808.2—dc23
LC record available at https://lccn.loc.gov/2021007127
LC ebook record available at https://lccn.loc.gov/2021007128

ISBN: 978-1-032-00380-1 (hbk)
ISBN: 978-1-032-00381-8 (pbk)
ISBN: 978-1-003-17388-5 (ebk)

Typeset in Stempel Garamond LT Pro
by Apex CoVantage, LLC

Dedicated to my brave and bold E and H.
Keep telling your stories. You will change the world.

Contents

Artistic Advisers	*xi*
Special Thanks	*xii*
Foreword	*xiii*
Introduction: Why Are We Here?	*xvii*
Prologue: How this Book Works	*xix*

1	Creating Compelling Characters	1
2	Writing Electric Dialogue and Silent Moments	15
3	Environment and Idea	26
4	The "Well-Made Play" (Short and Long Form)	34
5	Scene Structure	54
6	Monologue Structure	57
7	Thoughts on Aristotle's *Poetics*	64
8	Other Structures	68
9	Writing in 3D for the Living Stage	73

10	The Limitless Room	77
11	The Revision Process	87
12	The Business of Playwriting	97

Appendix A: For Further Study	*114*
Appendix B: Basic vocabulary, Formatting, and A Note on the Recommended Reading	*117*
Appendix C: Additional Worksheet and Writing Prompts	*122*
Appendix D: List of Play Recommendations by Chapter	*128*
Appendix E: Reading Pairing Recommendations Listed by Subject Matter	*137*
Appendix F: Reading Recommendations Listed by Publisher	*147*
Appendix G: Post-COVID-19 Online Theater	*159*
Index	*163*

Artistic Advisers

Jessica Bashline, University of Miami
Susan Bernfield, New Georges
Katherine M. Carter, director
Carrie Chapter, Temple University
Lee Edward Colston II, performer-playwright
Migdalia Cruz, playwright
Steve Feffer, Western Michigan University
Marcia Ferguson, University of Pennsylvania
Robynne Graffam, Germantown Academy
Gabriel Greene, La Jolla Playhouse
Yussef El Guindi, playwright
Allison Horsley, dramaturg
Margaret Laurena Kemp, University of California, Davis
Forrest McClendon, performer
Anna Morton, Roundabout Theatre Company
Amrita Ramanan, Oregon Shakespeare Festival
Lynde Rosario, Denver Center for the Performing Arts
Jackie Rosenfeld, Stephen F. Austin State University
David S. Thompson, Agnes Scott College
Michael Whistler, playwright-educator

This book was piloted in playwriting workshops run by Jacqueline Goldfinger at University of Pennsylvania and Jackie Rosenfeld at Stephen F. Austin State University.

Special Thanks

Chloe Aftel
Walter Bilderback
Nicole Cox
Christie Evangelisto
Shirley Fishman
Lawrence Goldfinger
Martine Kei Green-Rogers
Adam Greenfield and Jordan Harrison
Susan Gurman
Allan Havis
Allison Heishman
Stuart Hoar
Jo Johnson
Deadra Moore
Dee Moore
Dudley Moore
Sandy Pelham
Alix Rosenfeld
Barbara Spears
Paula Vogel
The Chateau Du Poigny Residency Family

This book was written in Philadelphia, originally the land of the Lenape.

Foreword

There was a time when I didn't know a thing about writing. That was yesterday. I'm not being facetious. We all go through that phase when everything we've learned about our craft is immediately of no use to us as we dive into our next play. The terrors, the doubts and insecurities, all the seemingly dumb questions we thought we knew the answers to, all of these feel as real and painful as they did the first day we set our pen to paper. We remember when we were absolute beginners, uneasy explorers of a world we investigated as we created it, each line of dialogue setting down the physics of a special, previously unrealized, and wholly thrilling place. In my process, I tumble into that state of abject ignorance every time I write another play or story, and I recall how fervently back then I wished I had learned to type. I still do. But more than that, I remember how I craved some essential workbook to steady me on my course, to keep me company in my struggle.

I had good teachers, professors who were professional playwrights with their own esteemed works to be proud of. Eugene McKinney and Glenn Allen Smith were my early mentors in my college days, though I regret not harkening to their instruction more than I did. I was studying acting in those days, all my lifeblood directed toward the actor's craft, and writing was a happy sidebar. But somewhere along the line, I fell in love with this playwriting thing, though my chaotic process was framed more by the things I'd learned as an actor than any dramaturgical approach. Still, I remembered and applied some of what my accidental mentors McKinney and Smith had taught me, and to some success. But I was working on a world they couldn't have imagined, because I could hardly believe it myself, and the stories and themes recklessly crashed into each other while characters bludgeoned one another with their clumsy lines, and it was a wonder that any of these works ever succeeded on any scale. In other words, I could have used this book.

For the beginning playwright, Jacqueline Goldfinger has crafted in her *Playwriting with Purpose* the perfect workbook. Within its pages are compiled dozens of exercises and writing prompts that deal with character development, scene structure, dialogue and subtext, idea and environment, and the ever-elusive central conflict. I can imagine how I might have made use of her chapters on the one-act and monologue construction and the elements of the well-made play. How valuable it might have been to encounter the probing questions she poses for the writer initiate questions I felt rumbling in me but could not ever phrase. And to find not just one but numerous exercises that wrestle with the notion of writer's block; these alone would have liberated me in those early dark stages of my process. I leaned almost solely on my own intuition then, yet this book supports and embraces that intuition as well, because Jacqueline's own experience as a dramatist infuses her book with the alchemical aspects of the writer's process. She knows there is no easy step-by-step formula. As she says, "Art is complex" and writing is about "transcending yourself" in order to "write your play the way it needs to be written." So appropriate then, that she calls on the wisdom of such diverse minds as Paula Vogel, Joseph Campbell, Gilda Radner, and José Rivera to guide us through the canyons of our complicated works. Through the scintillating counsel and insight of dozens of major playwrights and the inclusion of some of their most useful writing prompts, the beginning writers can start to piece together their own idiosyncratic vision for the birthing of their plays.

But this is a new age, and the art of writing plays has dramatically changed in the last 50 years, just as the culture has evolved and matured and flowered in ways we'd always hoped but couldn't quite imagine. Jacqueline adds to the catalogue of great works the contemporary geniuses of this new, vibrant age by listing for reference and exploration titles such as *The Laramie Project*, *Blown Youth* by Dipika Guha, *Off the Rails* by Randy Reinholz, and *Anowa* by Ama Ata Aidoo, among so many others. I revel in the knowledge that my mentor's name, María Irene Fornés, and mine are invoked as examples of particular approaches to theater that are unique and valued. It's clear that Jacqueline evinces joy in the declaration of these titles and authors, as if there's more on the menu than can possibly satisfy the palate, because as she proudly states, "a roomful of writers is still my favorite place to be." This book, to my mind, is the next favorite place to be.

It is her exultation that finally distinguishes Jacqueline's book from the rest of the pack. The manner in which she sometimes ends her sentences in exclamation points and declares in full caps, YOU CAN DO ANYTHING ON-STAGE, suggests a forceful love of this ageless craft. There is a passage in one late chapter in which her poem/prayer/chant bursts forth with all the fire of her writer's heart:

Amen!
Like Brother Williams, I write for love.
Physical love.
Emotional love.
Intellectual love.
Terminal love.
Fleeting love.
Love that makes characters break out into song.
Love that makes characters kill.
Love that wills dead characters back to life.

I suppose this is the reason I have made a life in this writer's room. It's **love** I seek between the lines and margins of my plays. Love for the ghosts that call me to their cause. Love for the ways we make community around stories that start with an empty page. Love of the empty page. A beginning writer like I used to be could hold hands with a book like this, but since I am always an absolute beginner, I may just as well hold hands with it now.

– Octavio Solis, December 2020

Introduction

Why Are We Here?

To the New Playwrights

If anyone tells you that they know the "right way" to create a new theatrical text, immediately turn around and run in the opposite direction. There is not one "right way" to create any piece of art.

Writing plays. Creating performative pieces. Jigsawing theatrical texts. All of these creative endeavors are wildly subjective processes that are unique to each individual. In fact, even an individual artist's processes might evolve over time.

So, I am not here to tell you the "right" way to write your play. I am here to give you a toolkit of creative screwdrivers and wrenches along with a sprinkle of inspiration. Once you finish this book, you will have a full creative workshop of playwriting tools that you can employ, or ignore, at your leisure.

In the future, you might use all of these tools in one play – or not. In the future, you might use these writing prompts again – either in this order or individually. My goal is to give you a future in playwriting, not to dictate what you write or your specific process.

The most important lesson I can impart is that You Can Write. You do not need anyone's blessing or grace. If you write plays, you are a playwright, and I am proud to call you a colleague. So just write.

Write for yourself.
Write for your children.
Write for your cat or your God.

If an idea stays in your mind, it will always be the perfect, untouchable, and unstageable idea. If you write, the idea might shift, the drafts might be lumpy and imperfect, but you will have a play that you can put on the stage and share with the world.

For me, it's in the magic of that sharing – the enchanting transition from page to stage – that makes all of the trials and tribulations of writing worth it.

For others, there are different reasons to write; there are those who find that writing is therapeutic, that it builds communities, that it creates careers, that it satisfies a creative passion, or that it strengthens their empathy muscles and gives them better appreciation for the world – whatever your reason, it is a good one.

Art is best used in practice, so practice it in the way that enriches you and your life. That, my friend, is the "right way" to create art.

Now, turn the page, and be gone from me. Read and Write and Welcome to Our World.

– **Jacqueline Goldfinger**

Prologue

How this Book Works

A Note on Using this Book

Successful writers work in a wide range of ways. Therefore, this book does not demand that you work in a particular way. Instead, this book offers you an opportunity to learn about, and try, a wide range of theatrical tools to see what works best for you.

In each chapter, you will read about and then practice elements of the craft of playwriting. If you begin with Chapter 1 and work your way through the book chronologically, then by the end of Chapter 10 you will have all that you need to begin writing a new play. If you are looking to simply strengthen or practice specific craft skills, you can also skip to those chapters. The lessons and writing prompts work both in succession and as stand-alone skill builders.

This book also gives you a list of plays to consider reading at the end of each chapter; all of them are published and accessible. These plays will give you more concrete examples of the craft lessons in each chapter. These texts are selected with the following metrics in mind: overall excellence, strong example of the craft lesson in the associated chapter, variety of aesthetics, diversity of styles and approaches, multiple modes of representation and points of view, and an international view of English language and bilingual (English + another language) playwriting today.

If you continue working through Chapters 11–12, then you'll also find lessons about how to revise your play and how to get it produced.

My goal is that you can use this book to take you from the idea – or even pre-idea! – phase and, by the end of the book, have a fully revised play that is ready to submit to development organizations or for production.

Now sit back, relax, grab a coffee, sharpen your pencil, and turn the page to take the first step into writing your next play.

1
Creating Compelling Characters

If you already have a story that you want to tell, wonderful! Let's explore the characters that will be telling that story. If you don't have a story in mind yet, wonderful! We are going to create characters to help you find a story to tell. This book supports those who come to the table with a story to tell, as well as those still generating dramatic ideas. However, we begin with character because, no matter what structure or form you use for your theatrical extravaganza, at least one character will be the heart and soul of your story.

What Are Characters?

Characters are the raw materials for your new play. You might be writing a short play, a full-length play, or an epic in multiple parts. Regardless, characters will appear in all of them.

Characters can be human beings. They can also be objects, animals, nature, imaginary creatures, or anything else you want them to be! There is no limit.

Regardless of the form characters take, it is their individual wants and burning desires that propel the story forward, create complication and conflict, and provide an opportunity to connect larger themes and ideas.

The one universal truism in creating compelling characters is that they feel something deeply and are compelled to act on it – whether it's a commitment to changing the world or a commitment to ignoring it, a commitment to make something happen or a commitment to prevent something from happening, whatever the cost.

A character wanting something gives us a reason to watch. We spend our time at the theater to see something happen within characters. What is happening within those characters must be externalized so that we can see it on-stage. This is one reason long-running shows like *Law & Order* are so popular – the characters either desperately want, or do not want, the crime to be solved.

In *The Science of Storytelling*, Journalist Will Storr wrote:

> In a stable environment, the brain is relatively calm. But when it detects change, that event is immediately registered as a surge of neural activity. It's from such neural activity that your experience of life emerges. Everything you've ever seen and thought; everyone you've loved and hated; every secret you've kept, every dream you've pursued . . . Unexpected change makes us curious, and curious is how we should feel in the opening movements of an effective story. . . . That is what storytellers do. They create moments of unexpected change that seize the attention of their protagonists and, by extension, their readers and viewers.[1]

Interesting characters with significant depth, who have active wants and are motivated by deep needs that can be externalized, create an engaging theatrical story. "The aim of art is to represent not the outward appearance of things, but their inward significance," wrote the philosopher Aristotle.[2] A primary way that we show our stories on-stage is by characters going after what they want while making increasingly difficult choices to reach their goal.

The one thing you absolutely must have to write a play are characters who want something. In order to know what your character wants, you usually need to know about their lives, their histories, and their passions. There are, of course, a few notable exceptions to this rule. For example, Harold Pinter did not dig deeply into his characters' backstories. He heard a few lines of dialogue, and then wrote forward, learning about the characters along the way.[3]

However, as a beginning playwright, it is good to practice creating specific character in detail. Later, you may choose to use this tool of Character Creation or not, but you will have it in your creative toolbox in case you ever need it.

"I understood, through rehab, things about creating characters. I understood that creating whole people means knowing where we come from, how we can make a mistake and how we overcome things to make ourselves stronger," said Actor Samuel L. Jackson.[4]

"Because the only reality is subjective," wrote Playwright Yasmina Reza.[5]

To help you begin creating a great character, answer as many of the following questions as you can about the character whose story you may be interested in including in your play. This will help you to begin exploring a character so that you can unearth their deepest desires and learn what compels them to make the choices that they do. The information that you uncover in this exercise might be directly used in your final play, or it might not. What is important right now is simply taking the time to learn more about your character(s).

> *Exercise #1:*
>
> You can create as many characters, or as few, as you wish. But I suggest that you create at least three to practice thinking through individual characters and to generate ample material to draw from for future exercises.
>
> (NOTE: If you are working from a character who already exists in a short play or other material, start answering these questions afresh. Pick your favorite aspects of that character and dig deeper. Don't be afraid if your character, or your idea of the character, evolves as you learn more about them.)
>
> Name(s):
> City of residence:
> Occupation:
> Age or age range:

Partner:
Kids:
Job(s):
Passion(s):
Favorite hobby or hobbies:
What is the character's biggest fear?
What is the biggest lie they have told and why?
What is their schedule for a workday?
What is their schedule for a day off?
Most embarrassing moment:
Favorite movie and why:
Favorite book and why:
Who was this character's first love?
Who was this character's first kiss, and how did it happen?
Description of home:
If their home were on fire and they could grab one object to save, what would they grab and why?
What does this character want out of life?
Is what the character wants out of life actually what they need, or is it good for them?
How would this character's obituary read?
How would this character want their obituary to read?

Writer's Block?

If you have trouble getting started, grab a magazine, rip out a picture that includes a person that appeals to you (even if you don't know why), and answer these questions about that person. That will help give you a jump-start.

Congratulations!! You've finished your first writing exercise. You've created at least one character. You have the raw material to write a play.

Think about or discuss with a writing partner: What did you learn from exploring your character? What did you already know? What surprised you?

Often we surprise ourselves while we are writing, and that's a good thing! That means that the character(s) are beginning to speak to us; get out of their way. Listen to what they are saying to you. You might find that what you pull out of your subconscious while writing your character is more compelling than what you originally planned to write. Be open to many possibilities, especially this early in the process. Each possibility is an adventurous avenue to explore; they give you many opportunities to journey down different roads of a character's possible experience in order to find the one you are most excited to write about.

You may or may not use all of these characters and/or all of these characters' specifics for your play. However, you now know your character and their world better, which will allow you to write a more compelling character with greater specificity.

One of the counterintuitive realities of theater is that the more specific your characters and their situations are, the more universal their stories become.

Playwright In-Sook Chappell said:

> I use a lot of acting exercises. The whole thing of really imagining the backstory of your character . . . Even if you don't need it for the play, you as a writer know your character and then I think little bits of detail will come out through the play that you are unaware of and that flesh out the character.[6]

Let's now take one of your characters' specifics and turn it into a monologue!

What is a monologue? A monologue is a long speech by one actor. By writing a monologue, you will move from understanding your character on a personal level to begin hearing your character's voice – which is a vital step on the journey to writing dialogue for your character.

Exercise #2:

Pick one character from Exercise #1. Write an unconsidered monologue – a monologue, from your character's point of view, that you write from stream of consciousness and don't edit yourself. Here are prompts to choose from:

(1) When a character learns a secret
(2) When a character faces a betrayal
(3) When a character wins (or loses) something they want

You are now getting to know the voice of your character. You are learning about what they care about, what drives them, and what obstacles they face.

Now, let's take the next step.

In fiction and poetry, the readers (audience) have the luxury of sitting down with a text at their convenience, taking it in at their own pace. They can flip back to earlier pages and re-read information that they might have missed or misunderstood.

However, in playwriting (performative writing), your audience is time bound. They must watch the performance at the allotted time from a specific location (seat, wall, standing, sitting), and they cannot easily look back to review information that they missed. Therefore, they must be able to see and hear your character's journey. If you want your audience to be able to join your character on their journey, they must be able to track it on-stage. This requires your character to take actions.

"Be sure not to discuss your hero's state of mind. Make it clear from his actions," wrote Playwright Anton Chekov.[7]

To see a character's action on-stage can mean a lot of physical activity or none at all. Action on-stage is connected to the actions that the character pursues in service of fulfilling their wants.

Action might be shared in many ways, including movement, dialogue, and how a character relates to an object or space on-stage.

Examples of on-stage action include:

- An angel crashes through the ceiling of a bedroom and forces a character to have a reckoning with

what they really believe spiritually before they will leave (*Angels in America* by Tony Kushner).
- A woman deciding if she's going to let an injured, unconscious person who might be dangerous stay and receive medical attention in her home (*Detroit '67* by Dominique Morisseau).
- A high-stakes discussion between a teacher and a student who hold opposing values, and if the student does not convince the teacher of their point of view, then they will be expelled from school (*Gideon's Knot* by Johnna Adams).
- A soldier trying to decide if he's going back to the war after returning home injured (*Elliot, A Soldier's Fugue* by Quiara Alegría Hudes).

In a play, actions usually result in the character having to make a choice – and that choice has a consequence. Then the character has to deal with the consequences of that choice, which leads to another, more important, choice that must be made.

In this way, plays can be seen as a series of actions that characters make, which force themselves or another character into making a choice. That choice requires themselves, or another character, to take an action and make a choice. And on it goes; the choices get harder and harder, with more and more heightened consequences, until the biggest choice has to be made – and that is the climax of the play.

The continual heightening of consequences is often called "stakes" or "raising the stakes" of a play.

We'll talk more about characters making choices and facing consequences while raising the stakes in the Structure section of this book.

To begin with, let's focus on one character taking one action.

> ### Exercise #3:
>
> Read your unconsidered monologue aloud to yourself or to others.
>
> We learn about character through their choices and actions. What *action* is popping out at you? It could be a big action, like a loved one dying, or a smaller action, like being brave enough to ride the bus to school by themselves. What is happening in your character's life that they feel connected to and that involves them taking action and making a choice?
>
> For example, here is a short monologue given by a Southern preacher in one of my early plays:
>
> > *I always blamed myself for the deaths of my sisters. I didn't pray hard enough or I didn't believe strong enough. My mother was convinced that God didn't want his sweetest angels subjected to this world. So He took them. Before they could be poisoned by- (gestures to the world around him). She made me swear an Oath that I would serve God, every day of my life, so that He would protect my sisters in heaven. It took me years to learn that my mother . . . she needed something to say to herself every morning, to help her get out of bed. It took even more years to under-*

10   CREATING COMPELLING CHARACTERS

> *stand that we should never confuse what my mother needs to believe from what God truly says. And that my mother shouldn't be blamed for what she created, but neither was it to be given credence as what God wants. And that in this small space – between what she needs and what He wants – lays all the world.*
>
> In this monologue, we learn why the character became a preacher, how he came to his point of view as a preacher, and the choice he made to serve God with an understanding of the fallibility of humanity.
>
> Now, it's your turn.

Review the character that you began exploring in Exercise #2. Write a monologue or scene that includes them taking that action, making that choice, and what compels them to do so. (What is a monologue versus a scene? See the Prologue for a refresher of basic vocabulary.)

Now you have begun exploring a character that will have one or more compelling wants, which will help drive your play forward.

> *Pro Tip:*
>
> If you have a character that you've created and that character could tell multiple stories on-stage, that's great! That means that you've created a character with a very rich life from which to pull conflict. However, it also means that you might not be sure which of their stories you want to tell on-stage in this particular play.

> I always recommend beginning with the story idea for your character, which has the highest stakes – meaning, the stories that would give your character the biggest success in their life or, conversely, risks their total annihilation.
>
> This is sometimes phrased as the "Why Now?" question. Why is this character burning to do this RIGHT NOW? By answering that question, you give your play a strong engine to drive the character for the entire play.

For the rest of this guide and workbook, I recommend that you use the character(s) that you created in Chapter 1 in future exercises. We will move forward to new exercises with the idea that you have completed pre-writing exercises for these character(s) and have those details about their lives at your disposal.

If you choose to move forward using additional characters with other exercises, make sure that you do a few pre-writing activities in order to get to know them. You will need that information as you move forward through the exercises.

Acting Teacher Uta Hagen said:

> Talent is an amalgam of high sensitivity; easy vulnerability; high sensory equipment (seeing, hearing, touching, smelling, tasting – intensely); a vivid imagination as well as a grip on reality; the desire to communicate one's own experience and sensations, to make one's self heard and seen.

12   CREATING COMPELLING CHARACTERS

Talent alone is not enough. Character and ethics, a point of view about the world in which you live and an education, can and must be acquired and developed.[8]

Published Plays to Read to Study Great Characters (Alphabetical by title)

- *born bad* by debbie tucker green
- *Cost of Living* by Martyna Majok
- *Death and the King's Horseman* by Wole Soyinka
- *The Glass Menagerie* by Tennessee Williams
- *How I Learned to Drive* by Paula Vogel
- *M. Butterfly* by David Henry Hwang
- *Tribes* by Nina Raine
- *Trouble in Mind* by Alice Childress

Note:

If you are writing short plays, there are numerous "Best of . . ." short play collections published every year. I suggest reading the most recent collections as well as longer plays. These short plays can provide examples of how to create a rich character in a short amount of time.

Some of my favorite published short plays are: *Airborne* by Laura Jacqmin, *Chester, Who Painted the World Purple* by Marco Ramirez, *The Sandalwood Box* by Mac Wellman, *I Dream Before I Take the Stand* by Arlene Hutton, *The Blueberry Hill Accord* by Daryl Watson, *Bake Off* by Sheri Wilner, *On The Porch One*

Crisp Spring Morning by Alex Dremann, *The Mercury and the Magic* by Rolin Jones, *Roll Over, Beethoven* by David Ives, *Not a Creature Was Stirring* by Christopher Durang, *Jimmy the Antichrist* by Keith J. Powell, *7 Ways to Say I Love You* by Adam Szymkowicz, *Baggage Claim* by Julia Jordan, and *A Moment Defined* by Cusi Cram.

Notes

1 *The Science of Storytelling* by Will Storr, Abrams Press, March 10, 2020.
2 *The Basic Works of Aristotle* by Will Storr, Modern Library; Reprint Edition, 2001.
3 Interview with Harold Pinter, *New York Times*, Arts & Leisure, 1979.
4 *Samuel L Jackson on Why You Should Raise a Ruckus and Make a Change* by John Naughton, *GQ Magazine*, July 2018.
5 *Desolation* by Yasmina Reza, Knopf, 2002.
6 *Playwrights Series: Character*, National Theatre, posted on YouTube on January 26, 2018.
7 *Letter to Alexander Chekov*, 1886, Penguin Classics, 2004.
8 *Respect for Acting* by Uta Hagen, Wiley; 2nd Edition, 2008.

2
Writing Electric Dialogue and Silent Moments

Dialogue

Dialogue is simply words spoken aloud – long words or short ones, in any language, with any inflection.

I like to think of strong dialogue as electric. Electric dialogue is dialogue that zings and pops because a character's desire is an electric current running through it. This idea helps me to make sure that my character is *doing* something with their language. If my dialogue is electric, then a character is using their language to go after what they want – even if it is in a subtle or roundabout manner. In good dialogue, there is a palpable electricity running through it that is powering the character's journey forward.

In acting lingo, Dialogue is Objectives filtered through Tactics. It means that what a character says in a scene (dialogue) comes from what a character wants (objective) in that scene and how they go after it (tactic).

Just like people, every character speaks their own language, which is informed by their experiences, which are informed by their race, class, ethnicity, city, state, country, family, and other factors.

Even when characters speak in heightened or stylized language, you can often still learn a tremendous amount about them by how they use words.

In addition, characters – just like people – shift the way they speak depending upon the location, occasion, and person with whom they are speaking. For example, if I am refusing a sandwich and I am talking to my sister, I might say, "Yeah, I find ham and cheese sandwiches so gross." But if I am talking to my boss, I might say, "No, ma'am, I don't need a sandwich today, but thank you for offering."

All of these considerations should be taken into account when creating dialogue; and this is a reason that doing your pre-writing character study is so important. By knowing how they came to be the person they are today, you will better understand how they communicate.

Typically, what happens is that as you write your characters and get to know them better and better through subsequent drafts, your dialogue will become more and more specific.

Pro Tip:

Unlike fiction or poetry, playwrights do not usually say the name of the emotion the character is feeling. Instead, playwrights show what the character is feeling through how a character speaks their words.

For example, if I am listening to a couple have a fight, their words might be written like this:

HER: I. Can. Not. Stand. You! Anymore!

Next, I can pretend that she's just annoyed, not in a fight, which might be written like this:

HER: Pu-leaze. I cannot stand you anymore.

Next, I can pretend that she is beyond angry and trying to get him to go away, which might be written like this:

HER: Icannotstandyouanymore!Icannotstandyouanymore!Icannoutstandyouanymore! Go away!

However, occasionally, playwrights will include a short indicator of what a character is feeling in parenthesis in order to make sure their intention is clear. For example:

HER: (sarcastic) I love you.

Exercise #1:

One of the biggest challenges of being a playwright is learning to write the emotions through the words. Let's practice!

Sit in a public space. Listen to conversations occurring around you. Write them down verbatim. Next to each sentence or fragment write the emotion that the person is experiencing. Ignore correct grammar when you are writing down their dialogue. Instead, use words, punctuation, space on the page, and any other means to capture both the words and the feelings behind the words on the page.

Once you have the literal lines down on the paper as you want them, now play with them a bit. How would you change the lines so the emotion behind them is different? Turn an angry line into a loving one or a serious line into a funny one. Have fun!

Now write a short scene or monologue with the character(s) you created in Chapter 1 where the character(s) tell the story of their most embarrassing moment, or we see their most embarrassing moment actually happen. Pay special attention to how their embarrassment, and all of the accompanying feelings, change their speech patterns and their behavior.

We were using this exercise on realistic dialogue (dialogue you'd hear in everyday life). If you want to write in an elevated dialogue style, you can do that as well. In the recommended plays that follow, there is a wide range of work that uses many styles of dialogue:

- *The Aliens*: heightened naturalistic dialogue
- *Arlington*: realistic dialogue mixed with a language of movement
- *Becky Shaw:* hyper-realistic dialogue
- *Bottle Fly*: poetic contemporary dialogue mixed with the language of music
- *The Danube*: dialogue layered over recorded dialogue and driven by the unspoken
- *Mud*: highly stylized dialogue
- *Hurt Village*: exceptional regional dialect
- *Indecent*: intersplicing dialogue with theatrical time shifts
- *Pass Over*: lean, stripped-down dialogue (a contemporary cousin of Samuel Beckett)
- *Pumpgirl:* monologue, strong dialect work

If you are not sure how your characters speak when you begin writing, that's okay. When we first begin writing, sometimes we have to try out a number of different styles and aesthetics. At some point, usually when you're going into the second draft, you'll have to decide which direction you are taking the play in terms of dialogue. Always just remember, it's only paper at this stage. If you take it in a direction that does not work, you can always set the paper aside and begin again. Play, have fun, experiment while you have the time and are still learning about your theatrical voice!

August Wilson said, "My early attempts writing plays, which are very poetic, did not use the language that I work in now. I didn't recognize the poetry in everyday language of Black America. I thought I had to change it to create art."[1] But he didn't. He embraced the poetry of the everyday and elevated it to a new level of artistic interpretation that became his signature style.

Regardless of the style that you embrace, what's important is that you communicate the information that you want the characters and audience to have in order for them to leave with the ideas that you mean to communicate.

Exercise #2:

Make a list of six types of people that you know. This is just brainstorming, so there is no pressure. For example: account manager in an office, pet-store owner, six-year-old child, etc.

> Select two of the characters.
>
> Put them in a scene together. They do not know one another. They each have a golden retriever that has gotten loose and run away. They both see a golden retriever, think it is their own, and collide. They argue over whether or not the dog, which they just lost again, is their own.
>
> The point of this exercise is not the conflict. The point of this exercise is thinking about how the worldview of a specific character influences how they speak, the words they use, the ideas they have, and the arguments they make.
>
> Plus, you now have two additional characters to work with in writing your play if you want/need them.
>
> Are you hearing voices yet? Good. That's the goal!

Silent Moments and Stage Directions

Just like in life, many ideas and emotions are communicated in nonverbal ways. It is important to give the director and actors a sense of what those unspoken moments are going to be on-stage in a final show. In early drafts, playwrights tend to overwrite unspoken moments. This is just us trying to draw the world and our characters clearly so that we can figure out what is going on in our play.

However, as we work through revisions, we think about what silent moments and stage directions exemplify our character's journeys – and which are just in the way. If you can slim down your silent moments and stage directions to the most important ones to tell your story, then you give your director and actors enough information to work with so that they will tell the story that you intend to be told (especially given that we often don't get to meet the directors and actors of all of our work). In addition, specifically and uniquely described moments of silent action also help clue readers in to your intention without having to see the entire play staged.

Stage directors can also give you the mood or tone for a play. For example, in my play *Bottle Fly*, I wanted to ensure that the tone of the singing matched the tone of the play. So I described the singer's voice as "K sings beautifully; flawed and raw but with an underlying grace." While "flawed and raw but with an underlying grace" is not strictly an action, it ensures that the action of singing is executed properly.

There are also writers who create a new punctuation vocabulary to help people read their plays; in the notes section at the beginning of their plays, they tell people how many seconds a beat should be, etc. See Annie Baker (*The Aliens*) and Suzan Lori-Parks (*Topdog/Underdog*) plays for examples of this type of punctuation choreography.

In addition, there are writers like Alice Birch (*Anatomy of a Suicide*) and Caryl Churchill (*Love and Information*) who often chose to use no stage directions at all. They allow the director and actors to craft their own version of the play using their words as a springboard.

> ### *Writer's Block?*
>
> If you ever get stuck writing dialogue, open the nearest play or turn on your favorite movie. Write down the first few lines of dialogue. Now, write a scene that begins with those lines. See where it takes you. This task will help loosen up your mind and move forward with your writing. Even Aaron Sorkin listens to the classic rock music of his youth to stimulate his imagination![2]

Subtext

Acting Teacher Konstantin Stanislavski said that "spectators come to the theater to hear the subtext."[3]

So, what is subtext?

Subtext is the conversation underneath the conversation two characters are having – the meaning behind the words.

How do you write subtext?

Start with a character in conflict in a scene (a character who desperately wants something but can't get it). Then write dialogue and action that indirectly expresses the character's messages, emotions, and needs. For example: a girl is asking another girl to the prom and is very nervous:

BECKY: Hey, hey, Anna?
ANNA: Yeah?
BECKY: I was, you know, thinking about, in the cafeteria today –

ANNA: Ugh, I know, what was that lunch they were serving us? Blah.

BECKY: Oh, yeah, sure, blah, I mean, I kind of like overcooked, but whatever, you know, they had the prom ticket sales table set up?

ANNA: Right. The prom. What an ancient ritual. Who needs a prom nowadays?

BECKY: Yeah, like, so old. But it could be fun. Maybe. If like, friends, go together, like really good good close close friends, and get a limo and hold hands, or not hold hands, or whatever.

ANNA: Uh, I guess?

As a reader or audience member, we can see that Becky is working to get up the nerve to ask Anna to the prom. Subtext can increase conflict and stakes without the characters getting into a huge fight. It also creates wonderful opportunities for a director and actors to show the story through activating an important question and infusing it with emotion.

> ### Exercise #3:
>
> Use the following ingredients to write a short scene chock-full of subtext. Think about how you can combine both dialogue and silent moments written as stage directions as well.
>
> Characters: Two characters that you've created through writing exercises in Chapters 1 and 2* – OR – a brother and a sister
>
> Location: Pet store

Conflict: Whether or not to buy a fish

*If you use characters that you've created in Chapters 1 and 2 and think you might use to write your full play, then do not worry about this scene actually being in the play. It might end up in the play, it might not. Regardless, as accomplished playwrights mentioned in Chapter 1, digging deeply into your characters will inform and strengthen your process when writing your play because you know your characters better.

Pro Tip:

If you are worried that your characters sound too similar, and that is a weakness of the story, then black out the names of the characters and give the scene to a friend to read. Can they distinguish which character is which simply by reading the dialogue? If not, you might need to work on each character's own "language" to make sure that they speak distinctly.

Published Plays to Read to Study Dialogue and Silent Moments

(Alphabetical by title)

- *The Aliens* by Annie Baker (silent moments)
- *Arlington* by Enda Walsh (dialogue and movement)
- *Becky Shaw* by Gina Gionfriddo (dialogue)
- *Bottle Fly* by Jacqueline Goldfinger (dialogue and music)

- *The Danube* and *Mud* by María Irene Fornés (silent moments and recorded dialogue)
- *Indecent* by Paula Vogel (silent moments, layering of dialogue and time)
- *Hurt Village* by Katori Hall (dialogue)
- *Pass Over* by Antoinette Nwandu (dialogue)
- *Pumpgirl* by Abbie Spallen (dialogue and monologue)

In addition, performance group rainpan43 (Geoff Sobelle and Trey Lyford) have a wonderful well-made silent piece titled *all wear bowlers* that tours internationally and also can be found on video online. It's a great example of how you can tell stories silently.

Notes

1 August Wilson. "The Art of Theater No. 14." *The Paris Review*, no. 153, Winter 1999.
2 www.vulture.com/2013/07/aaron-sorkin-loves-dad-rock.html
3 *An Actor Prepares* by Konstantin Stanislavski, Routledge, 1989.

3
Environment and Idea

Story Versus Plot
The story is all of the information that you have about the characters and their world, including things that happened before the play begins as well as things that happened off-stage.

The plot is only the sequence of things that happen within the play itself.

Theme and Idea
Like peas and carrots, stories and themes go together beautifully. You may have a theme now or you may not, but as you write your story, it is likely that your theme will emerge. Usually, the theme comes from your character's emotional need and final realization at the end of the play.

Tip: The theme is sometimes also called the "idea" of the play. It is the idea(s) that the audience takes home in their pocket to discuss over drinks later.

If you're having difficulty locating your theme, don't worry. Be true to your characters and invest in the story that you're telling and work on illuminating the theme during the rewrite process. It is boring to watch a theme. It is interesting to watch a well-told story with interesting characters; stick to the story and characters, and the rest will come. Sometimes, a theme might not appear until the second or even third draft.

Most writing teachers that I know recommend writing from character and situation, rather than theme, simply because plays based on theme written by emerging writers tend to be more didactic than theatrical. However, if you want to begin writing by using a theme, here are some prompts to get you started:

- My play is about:
- My characters care about this because:
- These events in their past made them care about this theme:
- My characters are in opposition because:

If you're writing from theme, always keep in mind WHY your characters care about the theme and HOW that affects their actions.

Theater is action, story, and character; lectures are theme. When you begin writing, let the characters illuminate your theme – don't let your theme control your characters. You may surprise yourself with the exciting complexities that emerge.

Exercise #1:

Pick an idea or theme that you care about. For example: feeding the homeless, serving as a volunteer, providing mental health care to everyone.

Now create a list of people who could be involved in conversations about that theme.

Select one character from your list.

Write a monologue that digs down into why the character cares about this issue. Does it have something to do with an intimate experience? With their family? With religion?

Once you can locate WHY they care, you can write a play about this person and their issue, which is engaging and complex. We go to the theater to see people in action because they care about something. Digging down into your characters helps you excavate a WHY which will help you form a compelling conflict.

Now:

Think about your character(s) from Chapters 1 and 2. Make a list of greater social and cultural issues that they care about. Keep this list close while you write. It will help inform their journey.

Writer's Block?

Make a playlist of songs for your main character. Listen to them once. Soak them in. Now, replay them. Type or write the lyrics as you listen. What do the characters want? What are their conflicts? Hearing – with both your ears and your hands – why a character in a song is singing can help inspire you to figure out the character in your play.

Genre

Genre is a category of artistic composition, as in music or literature, characterized by similarities in form, style, or subject matter.

Technically, every piece of work belongs in a genre – drama, comedy, dramedy, horror, sci-fi, and so on. Usually when theater companies say they are looking at genre plays, that usually means they want something in the horror, sci-fi, or another rare theater genre.

Exercise #2:

Genre exercise: Having fun with horror!

(1) Select a location:
   Condemned house
   Deserted train station
   Empty ballroom
   A cemetery
(2) Select a prop:
   Kitchen knife
   Baseball bat
   A poisonous liquid
   A wig
(3) Write a scene using the location and prop. The scene can be the more traditional "horror" aesthetic or a simply a spooky moment meant to strike fear in the audience within another type of play.

ENVIRONMENT AND IDEA

> Now:
>
> *Think about the genre of the play that you want to write with your character(s) from Chapters 1 and 2. Write down your options and ideas. You don't have to make any final decisions right now, but beginning to think about whether or not you want to write in a clearly defined genre – like horror or comedy or sci-fi – will help you define the story that you want to tell.*

Environment

We always must remember that we are writing for a work to be seen and heard.

Therefore, the Environment is a major element which helps audience members learn about the story and the character, as well as make assumptions about the journey of the play.

For example, if you set a wedding proposal scene at a baseball game versus if you set a wedding proposal scene in a romantic restaurant – then the audience will instantly know something about the characters, without the characters speaking a word.

Think about how the environments you select speak to your characters and their journeys.

> ### *Exercise #3:*
>
> Write a 2–3 page wedding proposal scene between two characters set in a football stadium.

Then write a 2–3 page wedding proposal scene between two characters set in an idyllic flowering forest.

Then write a 2–3 page wedding proposal scene between two characters set at Disney World.

Look back over these scenes and think about how WHERE they chose to propose informed us about aspects of their character, lifestyle, and priorities.

Now:

Go back and look at the list of spaces that your character(s) from Chapters 1 and 2 inhabit. Make a note next to the places that are the most meaningful to them, and why. If you have time, write short monologues about what happened at that space/why that space is meaningful for them, from your character's perspective.

Pro Tip:

Write What You Know – Or Not?

One question I get from students is if they should "write what they know." This is an old adage, and I don't agree with it. I think it oversimplifies the capacity of what writers have the ability to write well.

The saying goes back to Mark Twain, who wrote in *The Adventures of Tom Sawyer* and *The Adventures of Huckleberry Finn*, "Write what you know."

However, Twain did now follow the adage himself, and he wrote it within a fiction narrative. In fact, the narrator of the books is not the author himself but a young boy – Huck Finn – who has yet to learn the ways of the world. My guess is that Twain never meant for it to be taken literally and would probably be very amused that Huck's four-word pronouncement has become a noted sentiment in the literary establishment.

I say:

Write what you love.
Write what you are curious about.
Write what you are passionate about.
Write what you want to learn about.
Write from movement and impulse.
Write from rhythm.
Just write.

But if you do decide to write about a topic or people that you are not entirely familiar with, then make sure you do your research – and once you get into development, include dramaturgs, directors, and other artists who have experience within those communities or with those topics. This way you will make sure that you are writing a deeper truth and not slipping into stereotype or appropriation.

Published Plays to Read to Study These Topics

- *Anna in the Tropics* by Nilo Cruz (environment)
- *Anowa* by Ama Ata Aidoo (environment and idea)
- *Back of the Throat* by Yussef El Guindi (idea)

- *The Children's Hour* by Lillian Hellman (environment)
- *"Master Harold"... and the Boys* by Athol Fugard (environment and idea)
- *The Nether* by Jennifer Haley (genre/Sci-Fi and Mystery)
- *School Girls; or, the African Mean Girls Play* by Jocelyn Bioh (genre/Comedy)
- *Shopping and F*cking* by Mark Ravenhill (idea)
- *Top Girls* or *A Number* by Caryl Churchill (idea and genre/Time Travel/Futuristic World)
- *The Ugly One* by Marius von Mayenburg (idea)

4
The "Well-Made Play" (Short and Long Form)

The idea of the "well-made play" was codified by the French dramatist Eugene Scribe and the German dramatist Gustav Freytag in the 1800s. Later, a British version of this structure would appear in William Archer's *Play-Making* (1912), and an American version would be published in George Pierce Baker's *Dramatic Technique* (1919). This is the type of play that you will see on most stages in the United States of America, Canada, and Western Europe today. It follows a traditional Western storytelling structure:

- A clear and well-defined beginning, middle, and end
- Clear main character(s)
- A protagonist who is going after a goal (the PRO in protagonist simply means someone who is going after something, they are being proactive)
- An antagonist who is challenging or blocking the protagonist's journey toward their goal (the ANTA in antagonist simply means someone who is actively opposing the goal)
- In the early years of well-made plays, the writers made the protagonist the "good guy" and the antagonist was the "bad guy." This rule no longer applies.

However, "well made" does not connote that is "right" or "best" way to write a play. "Well made" is simply a term that connotes the structure of a play that follows a certain form.

Usually the structure for a "well-made play" is drawn as a triangle or a mountain shape. I think of it more as a gently sloping cliff that leads to a steep drop-off. Please use whatever visual is useful for you.

In addition, different vocabulary is used by different playwrights to describe each structural point within the play – the differing vocabulary words often mean the same thing. I've used multiple vocabulary options for each step in the structural process that follows so that you will not be surprised if you hear folks use a variety of language to explain the same thing in the future.

(1) **Beginning**: Introduction/Exposition/Status quo/Inciting incident
(2) Status quo is broken/inciting incident happens – life cannot continue as normal.
(3) **Middle**: Rising action/Mounting complications, protagonist actively goes after their goals, antagonist actively blocks goals, the challenges that the protagonist faces get bigger and bigger, the stakes get higher.
(4) **Climax**: The protagonist has the biggest decision to make at the top of the "well-made play" mountain. This decision often connects with the theme/idea of the play, showing us what the character has learned, or not learned, through the story via a decisive

action. (Sometimes called a "reversal" if the character and/or their situation change thanks to what they've learned on their journey.)
(5) **End**: Fallout of decision/Denouement/Return; if the character has learned something and improved themselves, then there is typically a catharsis at the end of the play. However, a catharsis is not required for the play to end.

When you look at the diagram of the "well-made play" that follows, or the description of the structure given earlier, notice that it is broken down into five clearly defined movements. Later, when you are reading or viewing plays, see if you can identify the five general movements of the piece. Are any of these five movements missing? If so, what is the impact on the story? What is the impact on you as an audience member? It is often easier to see structure in others' work than it is in your own. By practicing identifying how a play is structured and how it moves, you will strengthen your structure muscle. This will give you more information and power to work with when you sit down to write your own play.

The "Well-Made Play" Structure

We'll discuss the elements and structure of tragedy, which influenced the invention of the "well-made play" structure, in our chapter about Aristotle.[1]

Here are a few storytelling rules for well-made narratives:

The "Well-Made Play" Structure (begin on the bottom left-hand corner)

4: Climax

3: Middle-
A series of mounting challenges and complications which raise the Stakes for the Protagonist (typically 3/5th of play length)

Fall out of climax

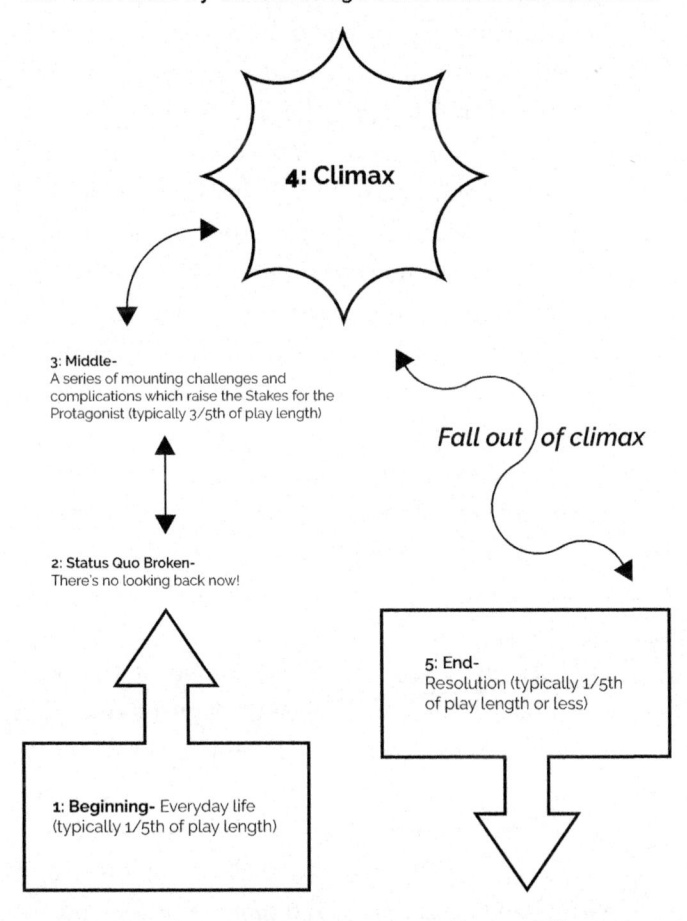

2: Status Quo Broken-
There's no looking back now!

5: End-
Resolution (typically 1/5th of play length or less)

1: Beginning- Everyday life (typically 1/5th of play length)

Figure 4.1 Graphic Representation of the "Well-Made Play" Structure

Credit line: Figure design by Rachel Goldfinger, HeyGoldfinger Designs

(1) The specific becomes the universal – the more specific you make a character and their situation, the more universal the story becomes. When you write

"general" characters and a "general" situation, the story becomes mushy and uninteresting.

(2) We admire a character's hard work and how hard they try, even when they don't succeed.

(3) Theme usually comes out of the decision(s) that your main character(s) make at the climax of the play and how they handle the fallout from the decision(s). Often, we might not know the theme or idea of the play until after writing a draft or two of it.

(4) Characters must be actively pursuing something, and that something must have personal importance (stakes).

(5) No work is ever wasted. Even if you do not use pre-writing or writing in your final script, knowing as much about your character and their world as possible will help elevate the complexity of the story on your page.

(6) You get one "buy" at the beginning of the play. One unbelievable thing. Then the logic of your play must make sense in the world that you create.

(7) Once you establish the rules of your world, be careful not to break them. If you break them, then either (a) it will feel like shallow, uninteresting writing and audiences will disengage or (b) you are breaking them for a reason because it means something specific and important for your play.

Short Plays

Short and one-act "well-made plays" typically follow the same rules as full-length plays. The only difference is that there is usually little to no exposition – we just jump right into the conflict of the play – and there is usually only one major complication in the middle of the play.

Exposition

Try to avoid overt exposition in your play, especially in later drafts. Sometimes, we need to write a lot of exposition in early drafts in order to fully understand the characters and the world. But then most of the exposition should be whittled away to simply what you absolutely need to tell the story.

Whenever possible, as Horace advised, begin "in medias res" meaning "in the middle of things" not "ab ovo" meaning "from the very beginning, or origin," of your story.[2] That way, you will limit any temptation to write a lot of exposition, and you will engage your characters more quickly in the complications of their predicament.

Also, remember that the middle of the story can be the beginning of the play (point of attack); in extension, it can be the beginning of your plot. As such, it will still reflect the beginning-middle-end structure.

> *Pro Tip:*
>
> If you need to use a lot of exposition in a moment (sometimes called an "exposition dump," the easiest ways to hide it are behind larger moments of comedy or disagreement.

Likability

Characters do not need to be likable, but they do need to be interesting. A great, complex character is always interesting to watch, even if the audience disagrees with them.

Dramatic Question

What is the central conflict for your protagonist(s) that will act as a through line for your play? For example, in *Romeo and Juliet*, will the young lovers get to be together in the end? While your play can have many conflicts and questions, plots and subplots, there is typically one overarching question that is uniting all of the stories in the play. This is usually the dramatic question. Some have referred to the dramatic question as your "compact with the audience," because it is this question that they know will frame the story of the play and be answered in the end.

Stakes

Stakes are what happens if the character fails or succeeds. We tend to be more interested in characters whose actions and conflicts have high stakes – whether those stakes be communal or personal.

An example of communal stakes: Saving the world! Superheroes!

An example of personal stakes: You only have one friend in the world, you're in high school, and you want to ask this friend to the prom. But if they reject you and you make them uncomfortable, you're afraid that you'll lose the only person in your life who really cares about you.

Director Peter Brook wrote: "A stage space has two rules: (1) Anything can happen and (2) Something must happen."[3]

> ### Exercise #1:
>
> Practice telling stories using the beginning-middle-end structure!
>
> Select your favorite fairy tale or myth.
>
> Retell it in one paragraph form:
>
> > First sentence should encapsulate the beginning.
> > Second and third sentences should encapsulate the middle.
> > And a final sentence should encapsulate the end.
>
> Do this a few times, with a few of your favorite stories. Now, make up a new story – or three or four or more! – in the same beginning-middle-end format using your character(s) from Chapters 1 and 2.

> ### Writers Block?
>
> Go to a visual art museum or open your favorite book of visual art. Look through the exhibit or book. What pictures look like they are at the beginning of stories – where the character cannot continue life the way it

THE "WELL-MADE PLAY" (SHORT AND LONG FORM)

> was? What pictures look like they are from the middle of a story – characters are facing obstacles, making decisions, and working to move toward their goal? What pictures look like they are from the end of a story – where a character has either succeeded or failed or made an unexpected change that ends that particular story in their life? Sometimes imagining stories in a visual manner helps activate new parts of our creative thinking and gets us unstuck. In addition, you might find visual images that resonate with your character's journey and write a monologue or scene where your character talks about why they connect with the piece. Whether or not you use that monologue or scene in your actual play, it will give you more information about your character which will help you get unstuck.

Conflict

Conflict is often confused with characters yelling at one another. While characters might be yelling at one another when they are in conflict, they might also be doing other things – like speaking quietly, moving items around into a new order, or simply standing still. True conflict is defined as a struggle between opposing forces, and you can show this struggle on-stage in many different ways.

Goals

What the character is going after. These goals can be physical, spiritual, or emotional. A major aspect of being a playwright is learning how to show these goals on-stage so that the audience can be a part of the character's journey.

Obstacles
What gets in the way of a character reaching their goals.

Action
What a character does to accomplish their goals.

Objective
A character's pursuit of a specific goal in a scene. Also referred to as the intention or driving question of the character.

Super-Objective
A super-objective focuses on the entire play. A super-objective can direct and connect an actor's choice of objectives from scene to scene. The super-objective serves as the final goal that a character wishes to achieve within the script. Another way to think about the super-objective is a driving character trait, so the overarching goal within the play would also serve the character's raison d'être.

Tactic
Tactics refers to the methods used to achieve goals. Usually, actors use a wide variety of tactics to create believable interactions. For instance, if an actor has the

goal "to threaten," then various tactics might be used to threaten; for example, an actor might yell at one point, try to kiss up to the other character at another point, and pull a gun on the other character at another point. All of these "tactics" (yelling, creating false empathy, pulling a weapon) make for a varied and interesting scene and build the stakes within the story.

Characterization

Putting together all facets of a character to bring life and interest to that character.

> *Exercise #2:*
>
> (1) Pick one of these spaces and write a description:
>   Parking lot
>   Living room
>   Boat
> (2) Now . . . a character of your choice is on a blind date. The space you just described is the first location where your character is meeting, or is escorted to by, their date. Write an internal monologue of your character's reaction to the space and what assumptions are made based on the space.
> (3) Now, write the scene from the blind date. In the scene, at least one, if not more, of the assumptions from your character's monologue are overturned.
> Now:
> (4) Think about the spaces that your characters (from Chapters 1 and 2) inhabit. Make a list of spaces

for each character – we may not see all of these spaces on-stage, but they would still influence each character's life and journey. Once you have your list of spaces for each character, jot down a few notes about how each character feels about each space. (Do they love it? Hate it? Are indifferent? Why? How does this space influence the way they feel or act?) Keep this list close to you while you write. It will help you write in "3D" for the stage. The concept of writing in 3D will be more specifically discussed in a future chapter.

Pro Tip:

You actually know well-made storytelling structure subconsciously if you are raised in the West. Everything from commercials to meeting agendas to children's books utilize all or parts of this structure. If you find it difficult to "think structurally," just relax. You've got this.

If you would like additional support, you can find a worksheet on structure in the Appendix.

Exercise #3:

Story Paragraph for a Full-Length "Well-Made Play"

If You Are Writing a Short Play, Skip to the Next Exercise

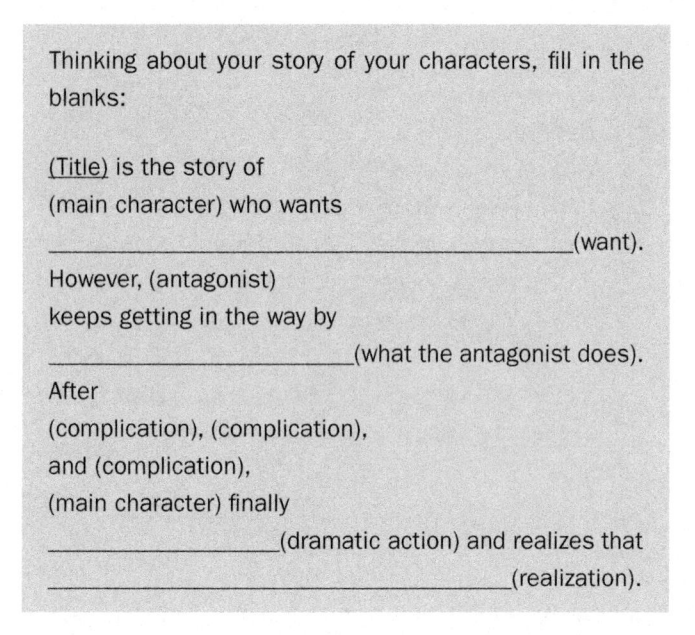

> Thinking about your story of your characters, fill in the blanks:
>
> (Title) is the story of
> (main character) who wants
> _____(want).
> However, (antagonist)
> keeps getting in the way by
> _____(what the antagonist does).
> After
> (complication), (complication),
> and (complication),
> (main character) finally
> _____(dramatic action) and realizes that
> _____(realization).

These blanks are the basic building blocks for structuring the plot of your story, so keep them handy. Also, the theme of your play will probably be connected with your character's realization and/or your character's need. When refining this paragraph, many other ideas, like specific plot points or character moments, might arise. Write those down on a separate sheet of paper. They might be useful when we begin the structuring process. **Please note, this is a very basic, very flexible tool that should help you keep your story on track (i.e., so you don't write 300 pages, but the play's story doesn't go anywhere) but it should not limit you, your story, or your imagination. Stay loose and have fun!**

DO THIS EXERCISE AS MANY TIMES AS YOU WISH. Sometimes, you need to brainstorm a few different stories to find the one you want to write, and needs to be written, right now.

Short Play Exercise: Five Steps to Writing a Well-Made Ten-Minute Play

Step 1: Beginning to Build a World

Atmosphere is extremely important in theater, and setting the right atmosphere lets the writer breathe life into their work and world. Choose one of the following items, and spend two to three minutes imagining the space. Then write a short paragraph (50–100 words) describing the setting:

Attic
Seashore
Heaven
Derelict building
Psychiatric ward
Inside a drainpipe
Deserted street
Apartment
Lifeboat
The sky

Step 2: Creating a Character Profile

Now it's time to populate this world with people. Think of a character that might be in this setting.

Answer the following questions, and write down any other detail that comes to mind.

I was born _____
My first memories _____
I remember my mother _____
I have been to _____
Since seven o'clock this morning _____
How do I feel about this setting? _____
I am in this setting because _____
I love _____
What interests me now is _____
I cannot understand why _____
I have been reading/watching _____
I wish _____

Step 3: Monologue

Now let's get to know a bit about your character's voice. Select one question from Step 2 and have your character elaborate on the answer. This monologue will probably never go into the play, but it will help you get to know your character better and begin to hear their voice.

Step 4: Other People in Their World

Now that you know a bit about your character, spend a few minutes answering these questions:

Who is their best friend and why?
Who is their worst enemy and why?
Who is their parental figure, and how do they feel about them?

Who is their partner (if they have one), and how do they feel about them?

Do they have children or other important person(s) in their lives? If so, who are they/what is the relationship/how do they feel about one another?

Step 5: Ten-Minute Play

You now have a world and characters for your play! Next, pick the secondary character who feels most in conflict with your primary character. This conflict should be over something specific and be deeply meaningful to the primary character.

Write a scene between them where they address this conflict. This scene might end up in the play, or it might not. It might be your first scene or your last. Use this as a way to get to know them and their world better so that you can write a strong play.

Once you've done all five steps, you will have all of the ingredients for a short play: space, characters, and conflict! Now write your play!

Reminder: General structure for most ten-minute plays:

Jump straight into the action – don't spend time setting context. Think about who your characters are and what they want.

Pages 1–2: Set up the world of the main character(s).

Pages 1–3: Something happens to throw their world out of balance.

Pages 3–9: The conflict escalates. Each time the main character makes a choice, it creates a new problematic situation that they have to make a choice about. Through this journey of escalating conflicts and making choices, the character learns something(s).

Pages 9–10: The character has one final major choice to make in the story. This choice illustrates whether or not they are going to act on what they've learned throughout their journey and change or choose to return to the status quo.

Choices are ACTIVE. Your active choice-making character is your main character.

Plays are meant to be seen, not read, so make sure that you are including actions and active choices that can be physically illustrated on-stage.

Acts and Act Breaks

One-Act Plays.
Two-Act Plays.
Three-Act Plays.
Four-Act Plays.
Five-Act Plays.
Eight-Act Plays?
Which structure is "correct"?

The answer is: they are all correct, and they are all wrong.

How many acts you have usually signifies the depth and duration of the conflicts within the play. Usually, the more conflicts and longer duration, the more acts you have. Whether you have one act or five, if you are working in the "well-made play" form, then the structure of the piece generally remains the same.

Act Breaks Versus Intermissions

Whether or not you choose to split your play into acts, you also might choose to include an intermission in your play. An intermission is a point in the play where the audience has the opportunity to leave their seats in the middle of the action, and the play on-stage pauses.

When I'm debating whether or not to include an intermission in my work, I ask myself these questions:

(1) Do we need an intermission to make a drastic set or staging change?
(2) How will the audience be impacted by this break in the story at this exact point in the story? Will it enrich their experience to have a break? Do they need time to process a lot of information? Or will it disrupt their experience unnecessarily, give them time to get ahead of the play, and lessen the tension?

Depending on my answers to these questions, I make a decision regarding including an intermission in the script.

Short Play Exercise: Sloutline (A Lazy Outline) for a Short Play

Answer these questions to help you think about what you'll write about in your short play.

How are your character(s) and their world introduced in an interesting, telling way?

What complicates the world or the character's lives?

What action is the character forced to take due to this complication?

What are the results of this action, and how do they complicate the character's world?

The solution to the complication spirals out of the character's control, what does that mean for them?

How does the character "fix" the situation, and where does your character end up (both physically and emotionally)? What is your character's final realization?

Write the closing moments of your play (dialogue, silent moment, action, whatever you feel the final moments before the blackout).

DO THIS EXERCISE AS MANY TIMES AS YOU WISH. Sometimes, you need to brainstorm a few different stories to find the one you want to write, and needs to be written, right now.

Published Plays to Read to Study "Well-Made Play" Structure

- *A Raisin in the Sun* by Lorraine Hansberry
- *Art* by Yasmina Reza
- *Cambodian Rock Band* by Lauren Yee
- *Detroit '67* by Dominique Morisseau
- *Glengarry Glen Ross* by David Mamet
- *Good People* by David Lindsay-Abaire
- *Milk Like Sugar* by Kirsten Greenidge
- *Shining City* by Connor McPherson
- *The Thanksgiving Play* by Larissa FastHorse

Notes

1 William V. Spanos. "Modern Drama and the Aristotelian Tradition: The Formal Imperatives of Absurd Time." *Contemporary Literature*, vol. 12, no. 3, 1971, pp. 345–372. *JSTOR*, www.jstor.org/stable/1207844. Accessed 23 October 2020.
2 *Ars Poetica* by Horace, Harvard University Press; Reprint Edition, 1929
3 *The Empty Space: A Book About the Theatre: Deadly, Holy, Rough, Immediate* by Peter Brook, Scribner; Reprint Edition, 1995.

5
Scene Structure

Scene structure for a "well-made play" is pretty straightforward. The scenes are just miniature versions of the overall "well-made play" structure, but at the climax of each scene, the decision that the character makes pushes the story forward.

The scene includes: a beginning where the status quo is broken, a protagonist going after something, an antagonist getting in the way of the first character's goal, a conflict, and a climax that leads the protagonist to make a choice that will lead to a new or heightened course of action in the next scene. And so on, and so forth.

You'll have a number of mini-plays within the overall full-length play.

Of course, this will not always happen in a first draft (or sometimes even in a second or third draft). But it gives us something to revise toward as the play evolves.

> ### Exercise #1:
>
> Pick the last line that someone texted you/sent you in an email.
>
> Turn that line into the first line of a scene set in a grocery store.

Write a scene that is a miniature version of the "well-made play" structure.

This probably seems like an unartistic, crude way to write a scene. In some ways, it is. But if it feels awkward now, don't worry. This is just practice. Once you learn the mechanics of scene writing, then you can take or leave the various structural elements – depending on what you are writing. It's like being an athlete; you have to practice the moves over and over for them to become graceful and necessary.

Pro Tip:

Structure is meant to help increase creativity, imagination, and adventure – not limit it. Think of the structure as a suitcase to carry your characters in so that you can take them anywhere and, eventually, share them with the world. It doesn't matter whether your suitcase is made by Versace or Walmart. It just needs to match the characters inside.

Exercise #2:

Brainstorm what could happen in the next scene. If the earlier scene was within a play, what are the choices/decisions/actions that could happen next?

Think about the two versions of your scene. Which moments, dialogue, ideas, etc. are most compelling? Which are the least compelling? Why? Practicing thinking in the well-made play structure can be challenging, but also useful for when you move into thinking more deeply about your own work. Whether or not you choose to use the well-made play structure in your work, thinking in these terms will strengthen the structure muscle in the brain – so you will be able to write well within the structure – OR – write well by rebelling against the structure and knowing what/why you are rebelling against.

Writer's Block?

Often when we get stuck during our writing, it is useful to think about what could happen in the next scene. Then cross off your brainstorming list what you know would never happen. That way, you have a list of possible scenes to draft and play with, which is a great place to begin!

Published Plays to Read to Study Scene Structure

- *Among the Dead* by Hansol Jung
- *August: Osage County* by Tracy Letts
- *Bengal Tiger at the Baghdad Zoo* by Rajiv Joseph
- *The Crucible* by Arthur Miller
- *Flyin' West* by Pearl Cleage
- *The History Boys* by Alan Bennett
- *Intimate Apparel* or *Sweat* by Lynn Nottage
- *The Lieutenant of Inishmore* by Martin McDonagh

6
Monologue Structure

Playwright Suzan Lori-Parks said:

> The writer has two kinds of faith: actual writing and sitting openly. Have faith in your personal effort or sweat. And faith in God, or whatever you want to call it. Then the voices will come. Faith is the big deal.[1]

Monologues are complex and layered. To stand with one character for a significant amount of time takes faith in both your writing and in the character themselves. Have that faith. Whether or not that monologue remains in the final play, by granting time to your character and their voice, you will gain intimate knowledge of the character that increases the texture and depth of your story.

Monologues take place in the past, the present, and the future all at the same time. The best monologues within a play give some background about the past, which a character needs to make a choice in the present, which will affect their future. Playwright August Wilson is the American master of the monologue. Read any of his plays, especially *King Hedley II* and *Fences*, to understand how monologues can inform, reveal, and help characters on-stage make active, compelling choices.

Playwright Paula Vogel says, "Art is the writer not having control, but the subject having control of the writer."[2]

The mythologist Joseph Campbell wrote, "The only way you can describe a human being truly is by describing his imperfections."[3] Storr follows Campbell's thought with, "It's this imperfect person we meet in a story and in life. But unlike in life, story allows us to crawl into that character's mind and understand them."[4]

Part of transcending yourself and truly getting into the heart and soul of your character, so they are in control of telling their story, is to know the characters very deeply. Monologues are also terrific pre-writing activities. They allow you to dig into a character to begin to understand what makes them tick, which will inform their conflicts and journey in your play.

> ### *Exercise #1: Monologue*
>
> Pick an image from a magazine that has at least one person in it – preferably someone you do not know.
>
> Take a few seconds to look at the picture and notice all of the details.
>
> Then begin answering these questions:
>
> > What does she want?
> > What really annoys this person?
> > What does she obsess about?
> > What does she worry about?
> > What was she thinking when she chose this outfit this morning?

What has she never accomplished that she wanted to?
Why has she never accomplished it?
What has never happened to him?
How does she feel about where she lives?
What does she secretly want that she could never say out loud?
What does she fear more than anything?
Ever killed anyone?
Ever stolen something?
Biggest lie ever told?
What items does she display in her bedroom, her private space?
What items does he display in his living room, his public space?

Brainstorm a list to answer each of the following questions:

(1) What do I want?
(2) Who or what stands in my way?
(3) How far would I go to get what I want?

Now, select one or two answers from the brainstormed lists to write a monologue; usually it helps if you have a character beginning a new journey. If you need help getting started, here are some prompts:

- First day of school
- First day of new job
- Day after having sex for the first time
- Day after getting married
- First day in own apartment/living situation

Write your monologue!

Alternative Exercise

If you have characters from earlier exercises that you want to continue working with, select a picture from a magazine that you think would resonate with that character. Write a monologue about WHY that images resonates with that character and HOW it would affect their thinking.

By alternating questions about the character's psychological state, wants, and needs with their physical wants, needs, and surroundings, we begin to spark connections between their internal and external worlds. This will be exceedingly important in writing your play because we have to show, on-stage, what they are going through – often using objects and surroundings as touchstones.

Writer's Block?

There is a popular myth that Tennessee Williams wrote out all of Shakespeare's plays by hand. They say Williams wanted to feel the curve of each letter, the fullness of each sentence, so that he could replicate it in his own voice.

I don't know if this is true, but I love the story. Often, when I get stuck on monologues, I will transcribe my favorite monologues from stage or screen. That helps me break out of my own brain and crawl ever so much closer to the brilliant brain of another writer. This shakes me out of my writing funk.

Fun fact: Williams is the model for the notion that writing is rewriting. He would create multiple versions of plays and revisit characters often. And his one acts are often trial runs for longer plays.

Exercise #2: What We Can Learn Through Exploratory Monologues

Now step back, put it away for a few days, and revise!

What have you learned about this character that surprises you? What have you learned that might be useful if you write a full play? What objects have you learned are important to them and why?

Pro Tip:

Here is an example of how you can discover an important object to a character then include it in the arc of the play:

> *Let's say you're writing a play where a woman is grappling with her mother's death. Her mother left her a heart-shaped locket, which the mother used to wear every day. When the mourning daughter first receives the locket, it is so painful for her to see, so she hides it away in a drawer. As time passes and the play moves forward, she begins to emotionally heal a little bit. So she takes the locket out of the drawer and hangs it on her mirror where she can see it every morning. The character does not have to tell us, with words, that she is healing,*

MONOLOGUE STRUCTURE

> *because we SEE it. We see her relationship to the locket change. We know that the locket represents the memory of her mom, so we know that it is growing less painful to be reminded of her mother. The daughter is beginning to heal. Then, at the end of the play, the daughter removes the locket from the mirror, fastens it around her neck, and smiles. She has healed. She walks out, moving forward with her life, with the memory of her mother now happy and less painful.*

The changing relationship of a character with an object that has been laden with a specific emotional burden can tell us all we need to know about the evolution of a character's inner life without saying a word.

I often think of important objects as baskets of meaning. At first, the basket is empty – so it is light and easy to carry – and as the play evolves, we begin to fill the basket (i.e., the object) with meaning. This way, when I go through my play and look at the objects used, I can tell whether or not I should keep them or discard them more easily; if an object does not have a specific meaning for a character, then I probably don't need it. In addition, the visual image in my head of a full or empty basket helps me decide if I can put the object to better use – for example, if there is an object that should be important to the story or character but I have not imbued it with any meaning (its basket is empty), then I probably should fill the basket with meaning for a character so that they are more complexed and nuanced, as well as have more dramatic ammunition for the story they need to tell.

Whether or not you end up using this monologue within a play, if you write a play with this character in it, you would know so much more about them and could write a more complex and interesting journey.

Published Plays to Read to Study Monologue Structure

- *Elliot, A Soldier's Fugue* by Quiara Alegría Hudes
- *For Colored Girls Who Have Considered Suicide When the Rainbow Is Enuf* by Ntozake Shange
- *Funnyhouse of a Negro* by Adrienne Kennedy
- *Let Me Down Easy* by Anna Deavere Smith
- *Mary Stuart* by Jean Stock Goldstone and John Reich
- *Master Class* by Terrence McNally
- *The Piano Lesson* by August Wilson
- *Three Tall Women* by Edward Albee

Notes

1. Suzan Lori-Parks. Goodreads Quotes, www.goodreads.com/quotes/tag/playwright
2. Paula Vogel. Goodreads Quotes, www.goodreads.com/quotes/65657-art-is-the-writer-not-having-control-but-the-subject
3. *The Collected Work of Joseph Campbell* by Joseph Campbell, New World Library; Third Edition, 2008
4. *The Science of Storytelling* by Will Storr, Abrams Press, March 10, 2020.

7
Thoughts on Aristotle's *Poetics*

Aristotle's *Poetics* is considered a foundational text of Western theater.[1]

I agree that it is a great foundational touchstone, one that teaches important storytelling skills prized in the West.

However, I like to remind theater-makers that *Poetics* is really just a fragment of a thought experiment written for students by a brilliant philosopher who was trying to break down the structure and nature of tragedy.

Aristotle was working on a greater document trying to define and explain the workings of story. For example, we know he also wrote about creating comedies, but that the document was lost.

Unfortunately, many teachers and writers have taken this genius thought experiment and turned it into a "must-do" or "drama checklist" for every playwright.

That is wrong.

And I want to remind you that it is wrong.

And if someone tells you that it is the only way to correctly write your play, then tell them to go jump in a lake.

Write your play the way that it needs to be written.

***Poetics* is a wonderful tool to help us understand the foundations of theatrical storytelling, but it does not, and was never meant to, restrict creative imagination.**

For those who haven't read *Poetics,* it offers Aristotle's thoughts on poetry overall as well as the six formative elements of tragedy. I've listed the elements next in case thinking about them is useful to the way that you create a piece of theater.

- Plot: Often considered the most important of the six elements for tragedy. Plots means the arrangement of the incidents that we see within the piece (not to be confused with the story of the piece, which is all of the incidents of plot plus what happens on- and off-stage to the characters).
- Character: Actions done that demonstrate a character's moral compass or personal ethics. Action is key.
- Thought: Thought comprises both the rational processes through which characters come to decisions, as represented in the drama, as well as the values put forward in the form of maxims and proverbs.
- Diction: The medium of language or expression through which the characters reveal their thoughts and feelings.
- Song: A major medium of language or expression that SHOULD be included in tragedy.
- Spectacle: The theatrical effect presented on the stage including special effects, props, set, movement, and other spectacular happenings.

Exercise #1:

Write a scene set at a local fair that incorporates all of Aristotle's elements. Write for at least half an hour. Really give yourself the opportunity to explore what the elements have to offer your storytelling.

Share your scene with a friend. Can they spot all of the elements? If so, great! If not, think about how you could have used the element(s) that your friend did not see more fully to make the scene more dynamic.

While you are creating your new work, it might be useful to use this idea of "elements" to break down your revision into smaller pieces. For example, where are the seeds of "spectacle" in the draft? Are they dramatically useful to the characters and story? Would you want to cut them, add to them, or make them even more spectacular to strengthen the storytelling?

However, you use the elements, never let them limit your story. Only allow them the space in your process when it is useful for you.

Published Plays to Read to Study Greek Mythology, Ancient Plays, and Aristotelian Structure

- *By the Bog of Cats* by Marina Carr, based on *Medea* mythology
- *Electra/Elektra* by Euripides, translated by Anne Carson

- *Electricidad* by Luis Alfaro, based on *Elektra* by Euripides
- *Eurydice* by Sarah Ruhl, based on *Eurydice* mythology
- *Iphigenia Crash Land Falls on the Neon Shell That Was Once Her Heart (a Rave Fable)* by Caridad Svich, based on *Iphigenia at Aulis* by Euripides
- *The Seven* by Will Power, based on *Seven Against Thebes* by Aeschylus (not published but videos available online)

Note

1 The Project Gutenberg Ebook of *Poetics* by Aristotle, www.gutenberg.org/files/1974/1974-h/1974-h.htm

8
Other Structures

"We can only do what is possible for us to do. But still it is good to know what the impossible is," said María Irene Fornés,[1] who is often called one of the godmothers of contemporary American theater, along with Ntozake Shange, for their innovative use of language, structure, and idea which shaped a new generation of playwrights in the 1970s and beyond.

The type of plays that we have been discussing in this book are what you will see on most Western stages – the "well-made play" structure. However, there are many other types of structures used in performance, both on- and off-stage.

As Playwright José Rivera says,

A play must be organized. This is another word for structure. You organize a meal, your closet, your time – why not your play? . . . Theatre is the explanation of life to the living. Try to tease apart the conflicting noises of living, and make some kind of pattern and order. It's not so much an explanation of life as much as it is a recipe for understanding, a blueprint for navigation, a confidante with some answers, enough to guide you and encourage you, but not to dictate to you.[2]

What will the organizing principal – i.e., structure – of your play be?

Sometimes you will know this from the beginning of the process. Sometimes you will learn this through writing and workshops.

Here are a few other types of structure that you can dive into:

- Episodic: Plot begins early in the play, and then gently connected plots and subplots grow from and between characters; Think: Shakespeare, Juana Inés de la Cruz, Lope de Vega.
- Ritual and Pattern: Repetitions and reenactments help moments and movements acquire special meaning; Think: The Olympic Ceremony, Catholic Mass, Meditation.
- Serial Structure: Central theme holds a single entertainment together; Think: A Musical Review, Master of Ceremonies at an awards show.
- Chronological Structure: A time sequence bound performance; Think: A scavenger hunt, A computer game that requires you to complete one level in a certain sequence before moving on.

Also...

Experimental and Avant-Garde Work: While these are not specific structures, they typically are created out of an interest in bucking traditional structures and storytelling elements; Think: Matana Roberts, Richard Maxwell, Marina Abramovic, Fay Victor.

Of course, art is complex. You can see elements of one type of structure within the structure of another. As Composer Claude Debussy said: "Works of art make rules; rules do not make works of art."[3]

> ### *Exercise #1: Your Play*
>
> Begin writing your own play! Short or long, any genre. I know that writing an entire play, long or short, can seem overwhelming. However, if you break the writing down into small parts, then it feels more manageable. There are a few tips for how to manage your writing time in the next two chapters.
>
> If you've completed all of the writing exercises in this book, then you have the Who, What, When, and Why of your characters. Now you just need to decide How to write their journey in your play. And that's up to you. I can't tell you How to write your character's journey and the story of your play, nor should I. However, I will say, you are off to a great start!
>
> If you've created character(s) with depth and complexity, there might be multiple stories that these character(s) can tell. That's a good sign! While it might take you a little longer to sort out what the plot of your play will be, this means that you have characters that are more likely to be compelling to your audience and producers.
>
> My recommendation is to now either simply begin writing and find out where these fabulous characters in this interesting space with all of these passions and ideas take you.

If you have difficulty starting to write, go through your writing prompts and pick one that resonates with you. Write or revise a scene based on whatever resonates with you within the prompt response which you originally penned. It might be the first scene of your new play, it might be the fourth, it might not appear in the final first draft at all, but it will get you on the path to writing your play.

Break all the legs!!

Pro Tip:

Perhaps commit to writing ten pages per week at first. By the end of the month, you'll have a draft of at least one short play or a great start on a full-length play. If you continue this pattern, then you will generate pages and plays at a wonderful clip. Often the trick with playwriting is consistency, rather than waiting for the muse to inspire you.

Also remember: first drafts are just and only that – first. They are the immediate spillage from your brain. Don't judge yourself too harshly. Don't be too critical. You're going to revise the pages anyway, so just get the ideas in your head out onto the page – no matter how shapeless and weird they might look. Having a first draft, no matter how messy, gives you something to work with, and it will move your process forward.

Published Plays to Read to Study Other Structures

- *Ain't No Mo'* by Jordan E. Cooper*
- *Booty Candy* by Robert O'Hara
- *Chekhov Lizardbrain* by Pig Iron Theatre Company
- *The Colored Museum* by George C. Wolfe
- *Futurity* by César Alvarez with The Lisps
- *Revolt. She Said. Revolt Again.* by Alice Birch
- *Shock Treatment* by Karen Finley
- *Snow in Midsummer* by Frances Ya-Chu Cowhig
- *That Pretty Pretty; or, The Rape Play* by Sheila Callaghan
- *Untitled Feminist Show* by Young Jean Lee
- *Water & Power* by Culture Clash
- *The Wild Duck* by Henrik Ibsen

*Awaiting publication

Notes

1 *Promenade and Other Plays,* by María Irene Fornés, PAJ Publications, July 1, 2001.
2 *36 Assumptions About Playwriting* by José Rivera, 2020, https://howlround.com
3 "Claude Debussy Quotes." *BrainyQuote.com*. BrainyMedia Inc, 2020. September 28, 2020, www.brainyquote.com/quotes/claude_debussy_204267

9
Writing in 3D for the Living Stage

Writing in 3D

Remember that plays are telling stories in 3D.

Playwriting is a mash-up of visual, movement, and literary arts.

An audience will learn as much about the story from what they see physically on the stage as they do from what the character says or does not say.

For example, if a character says a line, and we see them do the opposite thing on the stage, then we'll think the character is a liar.

Some of the most exciting visual moments on-stage come from a playwright's personal experience, which they put on-stage. Let's generate some memorable visual moments that we can use as inspirations in our work.

> ### Exercise #1:
> List your top-five most memorable visual moments in the art (from any form: theater, films, visual art, etc.) and your top-five most memorable visual experiences in life. Do this quickly. Do not overthink them. Write what first comes to mind.

> Now, think about what makes these visual moments memorable. Was a special connection made? A life-altering realization? Just a purely beautiful moment? Jot a few notes next to each about (1) how you felt/responded in the moment and (2) how you feel/respond to it now as you have perspective on the event.
>
> Then think about the memorable moments in your three characters' lives. Often, one of these memorable moments will happen early on in the play and set the character on their journey of the play, and one will happen late in the play when the character has a defining moment/realization or makes a final choice.
>
> Look over the character creation exercise, scanning for possible memorable and important moments. Jot down a list of possibilities to use as fodder while you write and also to get you unstuck if you get stuck.

Navigating Feedback

Playwright Romulus Linney said: "There are three primal urges in human beings; food, sex, and rewriting someone else's play."[1]

Giving feedback on a play is challenging. Since playwriting is rooted in both performance and literature, most plays have to work both on the stage and on the page – hence the idea of writing in 3D. Most people, even incredibly smart folks, have difficulty "hearing" the play simultaneously as a work of literature and a work of performance when they read it.

In addition, the best feedback givers are not only nuanced, multi-stream readers but they also have a vision to see the possibilities of a piece.

I highly recommend using Liz Lerman's Guidelines to Critical Response (see the Appendix). Lerman's Guidelines helps us re-focus feedback from what the reader wants to what the artist wants to create with the support of the reader. In addition, it requires that readers/audience members let the playwright know what is working versus what is not working. Giving their opinion on both topics helps the playwright know where the "heat" of the play is (i.e., what is exciting and engaging) versus where the play is cool (i.e., what is confusing in a negative way or possibly unnecessary). This way, when a playwright sits down to revise, they do not throw out what is working as well as what is not working; they don't throw out the baby with the bathwater, as my grandmother would say.

I recommend that you keep all of your notes and pages. If you're writing on a computer, "Save As" every day and then save the new day's writing as "TITLE DATE"; this way, you never lose anything. You have all of the work that you've done accessible at any time. This will allow you to revise freely, cut and paste, delete and save, and not worry about losing any precious work. If you accidently cut a section that you later want to re-insert, all you have to do is copy and paste it from an older draft. In addition, sometimes you have an idea in one play that might not fit into that play – perhaps it is a play itself. You can confidently remove it from your current play and know that it is always there waiting for you when you wish to begin a new project.

There are as many views on the intent and responsibilities of the work as there are artists. One of my favorites is Playwright and Lyricist Lin-Manuel Miranda's reflection on the creation of *Hamilton*:

> My only responsibility as a playwright and a storyteller is to give you the time of your life in the theatre. I just happen to think that with Hamilton's story, sticking close to the facts helps me. All the most interesting things in the show happened.[2]

Published Plays to Read to Study Theatricality

- *9 Parts of Desire* by Heather Raffo
- *Blasted* by Sarah Kane
- *El Grito del Bronx* by Migdalia Cruz
- *The Elaborate Entrance of Chad Deity* by Kristoffer Diaz
- *Curse of the Starving Class* by Sam Shepard
- *Is God Is* by Aleshea Harris
- *The Language Archive* by Julia Cho
- *Lydia* by Octavio Solis
- *R.U.R.* by Karel Capek

Notes

1 *Six Plays* by Romulus Linney, Theatre Communications Group, 1993
2 *Gmorning, Gnight!: Little Pep Talks for Me & You* by Lin-Manuel Miranda, Random House; Illustrated Edition, 2018.

10
The Limitless Room

Dominique Morisseau said, "Everyone deserves to have their story fully told."[1]

While you are writing, here is a bit more inspiration to help keep you going. . .
YOU CAN DO ANYTHING ON-STAGE.
Say it again. Louder.
YOU CAN DO ANYTHING ON-STAGE!

To me, theater is a Limitless Room. It is a room with no walls, no ceiling, and no floor. It is a place where there is space for everyone. In this room, imagination is a rolling coaster, a yellow brick road, and a spiral seashell. It believes in you, even when you might not believe in it.

You can turn a classic into a robot play (*Heddatron*)[2] or a therapy session into a sensational theatrical experience (*Slave Play*).[3]

You can go on epic role-play adventures (*She Kills Monster*)[4] and animate memes (*Woman Laughing Alone with Salad*).[5]

You can dance with the devil (*Dr. Faustus*)[6] and memorialize a moment that changed American history (*The Laramie Project*).[7]

While most playwrights learn the tools and rules of the trade, some of the most thrilling moments in the theater are when they cast them aside and create worlds with their own internal logic. They move us. They make us squirm uncomfortably or connect with our own inner power.

F. Sionil José said:

> The heart of the theater is the play itself, how it dramatizes life to make it meaningful entertainment. To achieve depth and universality, the playwright must subject himself to intense critique, to know human character and behavior, and finally to construct art from the most mundane of human experience.[8]

Sarah Ruhl said: "Don't make a wall of glass between your play and the people watching. Don't forget they were once children, who enjoyed being read to, or sung to sleep."[9]

Daisaku Ikeda said: "The power of art can break the shackles that bind and divide human beings."[10]

Exercise #1:

Once You've Found a Story to Tell

What story do you need to tell? What are you dying to yell on a street corner? What haunts you when you can't sleep at night? And how do you transform these emotions, fragments, and ideas into a riveting dramatic narrative?

If you have a story impulse, list 12 adjectives (or short descriptive phrases) that describe your impulse.

Then, put these adjectives aside for later. Think of them as a stripped-down version of your subconscious, and return to them as needed to help you remember what passions fueled your initial inspiration.

Exercise #2:

Story Web

Think of this next exercise as a guided brainstorming activity to help you build your plot and character.

Go back and look at the Character Development exercises. You've already begun to create a great world for your story. Part of good storytelling is being able to use every detail you create.

For example, if your main character is a thief, then perhaps she gets a job in a jewelry store to learn how security works, so she can rob another store. This way, you are using one part of her life (her job) to inform the primary story in your play (a bank robbery).

A Story Web (details of story and character that connect to and bolster one another) will help you use every detail to feed back into the story and create a stronger play.

Right now, we only have a few details of character and story. Let's use these details to expand the universe of our story.

Next, list your main character's occupation, city of residence, and antagonist. Find ways these aspects of your character's life are connected, then continue your brainstorming. What other details can you discover about your character and story? If you get stuck, refer back to the previous exercises. Pick three more details of the characters life, and consider how they are connected.

Most likely, you won't use all of the ideas but will pick the ones you like best to use in your play.

Exercise #3:

Primary Moments Exercise

Many times, writers have a pastiche of images, moments, and bits of dialogue floating around in their imagination that connect with a certain story they need to tell. Often, these are the most dramatic moments of their story. Make sure to write them down and keep them in a file somewhere, so you don't forget them.

These primary moments are especially useful to have on hand when you get stuck or have writer's block, because you can throw one into a scene just to see what will happen. Even if it doesn't make any sense for a full play, it can help shake up your brain and get you unstuck.

"I wanted a perfect ending. Now I've learned, the hard way, that some poems don't rhyme, and some stories don't have a clear beginning, middle, and end. Life is about not knowing, having to change, taking the moment and making the best of it, without knowing what's going to happen next. Delicious Ambiguity," said Gilda Radner.[11]

Pro Tip:

If you are having trouble disciplining yourself to sit down and write, then this process might help you: Set a kitchen timer to 25 minutes, write for 25 minutes straight (no researching, no checking email, just write) then take a 5-minute break. Repeat. After doing this cycle three times in a row, then the fourth time through write for 25 minutes, but then take a 15-minute break. Then go back to 25-minute writing/5-minute break for three more rotations, and then after the fourth rotation, take another 15-minute break. So, your writing schedule looks like this:

1:00–1:25 Write
1:25–1:30 Break
1:30–1:55 Write
1:55–2:00 Break
2:00–2:25 Write
2:25–2:30 Break
2:30–2:55 Write
2:55–3:10 Break
3:10–3:35 Write
3:35–3:40 Break
3:40–4:05 Write
4:05–4:10 Break
4:10–4:35 Write

> 4:35–4:40 Break
> 4:40–5:05 Write
> 5:05–5:10 Break
> 5:10–5:35 Write
> 5:35–5:50 Break
>
> Continue this writing schedule for as long as you have time. This will keep you disciplined and moving forward on your work.

Following are 75 plays from around the world that remind us that one person's art is another person's snooze-fest, and no one can define what a "good play" is for everyone. And that lack of definition is what makes art a beautiful, precious, and powerful force in the world.

Read what looks interesting to you, ignore what doesn't. Throw in plays that excite you, befuddle you, and make you laugh. Just read and watch theater as much as possible. These actions will open your world to the beautiful possibility of the stage – just like your character's actions will shape their views and journey through the world that you create for them.

Following are very general categories; many of these pieces cross multiple categorial lines:

(in alphabetical order by title)

Wild Theatrical Rides
- *Angels in America* by Tony Kushner
- *Big Love* by Chuck Mee

- *Blown Youth* by Dipika Guha (theater for young audiences)
- *The Body of an American* by Dan O'Brien
- *Caught* by Christopher Chen
- *Collective Rage: A Play in 5 Betties* by Jen Silverman
- *Dublin by Lamplight* by Michael West
- *Failure: A Love Story* by Phillip Dawkins
- *Fairview* by Jackie Sibblies Drury
- *The Fever* by Wallace Shawn
- *Girl Under Grain* by Karen Hartman
- *Goodnight Desdemona, Good Morning Juliet* by Ann-Marie McDonald
- *In Love and Warcraft* by Madhuri Shekar (stage and virtual editions)
- *Kid Simple* by Jordan Harrison
- *The Realistic Jones* by Will Eno
- *Sagittarius Ponderosa* by MJ Kaufman
- *She Kills Monsters* by Qui Nguyen (stage and virtual editions)
- *The Skin of Our Teeth* by Thornton Wilder
- *Slave Play* by Jeremy O. Harris
- *Suicide Forest* by Haruna Lee
- *Underground Railroad Game* by Jennifer Kidwell and Scott R. Sheppard with Lightening Rod Special
- *Woyzeck* by Georg Buchner

Narrative-Focused Plays

- *2.5 Minute Ride* by Lisa Kron
- *Amadeus* by Peter Shaffer

- *The Amen Corner* by James Baldwin
- *Arcadia* by Tom Stoppard
- *B* by Guillermo Calderón
- *Blood and Gifts* by J.T. Rogers
- *Blood Wedding* by Federico Garcia Lorca
- *Bulrusher* by Eisa Davis
- *Crooked Parts* by Azure Osborne-Lee
- *Dutchman* by Amiri Baraka
- *Dr. Faustus* by Christopher Marlowe
- *Eight Gigabytes of Hardcore Pornography* by Declan Greene
- *Enfrascada* by Tanya Saracho
- *The First Deep Breath* by Lee Edward Colston II*
- *Fleabag* by Phoebe Waller-Bridge
- *Fuenteovejuna* by Lope de Vega
- *This Heaven* by Nakkiah Lui
- *Hir* by Taylor Mac
- *Holy Ghosts* by Romulus Linney
- *How We Got On* by Idris Goodwin (theater for young audiences)
- *The House of Desires* by Sor Juana Inés de la Cruz
- *In the Blood* by Suzan-Lori Parks
- *The Invisible Hand* by Ayad Akhtar
- *Last Night and the Night Before* by Donnetta Lavinia Grays*
- *Last Summer at Bluefish Cove* by Jane Chambers
- *Marisol* by José Rivera
- *Mauritius* by Theresa Rebeck
- *Mojo* by Jez Butterworth
- *Moon for the Misbegotten* by Eugene O'Neill
- *'Night Mother* by Marsha Norman

- *Off the Rails* by Randy Reinholz*
- *Oohrah!* by Bekah Brunstetter
- *Proof* by David Auburn
- *Skin Tight* by Gary Henderson
- *A Soldier's Play* by Charles Fuller
- *Stick Fly* by Lydia Diamond
- *Nora: A Doll's House* by Stef Smith
- *The Sisters Rosenweig* by Wendy Wasserstein
- *Teenage Dick* by Mike Lew
- *Trifles* by Susan Glaspell
- *Vincent in Brixton* by Nicholas Wright
- *Waiora* by Hone Kouka
- *The Whale* by Samuel Hunter
- *What the Constitution Means to Me* by Heidi Schreck
- *You Got Older* by Clare Barron

Commentary-Focused Plays

- *America v. 2.1: The Sad Demise & Eventual Extinction of The American Negro* by Stacey Rose*
- *The Cherry Orchard* by Anton Chekhov
- *Dead and Breathing* by Chisa Hutchinson (theater for young audiences)
- *Firebird Tattoo* by Ty Defoe
- *Galileo* by Bertolt Brecht
- *The Garden Party* by Václav Havel
- *God's Country* by Steven Dietz
- *Good Goods* by Christina Anderson
- *Heddatron* by Elizabeth Meriweather
- *The Internationalist* by Anne Washburn

- *La Ruta* by Isaac Gómez*
- *The Laramie Project* by Tectonic Theater Project
- *Machinal* by Sophie Treadwell
- *Mississippi Goddamn* by Jonathan Norton
- *P'yongyang* by In-Sook Chappell
- *Paul* by Howard Brenton
- *The Radicalisation of Bradley Manning* by Tim Price
- *Silent Sky* by Lauren Gunderson
- *Sugar in Our Wounds* by Donja Love
- *Underground* by Lisa B. Thompson
- *Until the Flood* by Dael Orlandersmith

*Awaiting publication

Notes

1. "Dominique Morisseau's Star Rises." *LA Times, Arts & Entertainment,* August 23, 2018.
2. By Elizabeth Merriweather
3. By Jeremy O. Harris
4. By Qui Nguyen
5. By Sheila Callaghan
6. By Christopher Marlowe
7. By Tectonic Theater Project
8. "F. Sionil José Quotes." *BrainyQuote.com.* BrainyMedia Inc, 2020. September 28, 2020, www.brainyquote.com/quotes/f_sionil_jose_620829
9. *100 Essays I Don't Have Time to Write. . .* by Sarah Ruhl, Farrar, Straus and Giroux; Reprint edition, September 15, 2015.
10. "Daisaku Ikeda Quotes." *QuoteMaster.Org,* www.quotemaster.org/author/Daisaku+Ikeda
11. *It's Always Something*, by Gilda Radner, Simon & Schuster; 20th Anniversary, Revised ed. Edition, 2009.

11
The Revision Process

Author Ernest Hemingway famously said: "The only kind of writing is rewriting."[1]

Revision can be more difficult than writing the original draft.

When you're writing the original draft, the world is your oyster. You can throw in everything, including the kitchen sink, your favorite dragon, and the kid next door.

I cram my first drafts full of everything that I want to be in the play. It is messy and inconsistent and full of contradictions.

The second, third, and additional drafts – those are full of everything that The Play needs to be in the play.

I am a midwife in the revision process; my job is to listen, think, and release my ego to allow the play to become the story it needs to be.

Playwright Jessica Huang said, "Doubt yourself. Trust the play."[2]

The revision process takes more discipline and a greater knowledge of craft. Revision is what takes a great idea for a play and elevates it to an actual great play. Your play might need two drafts to be ready for the stage, or it might need ten. You might want to begin writing draft two on a blank page, or you might want to begin with a scene that you like and revise it first.

Since plays must do double duty and work both on the page and on the stage, get the words in the air as soon as you can so that you can determine what is, and is not, working for you – whether that is by inviting friends over for snacks and a reading or by sitting in a formal workshop setting.

Often, writers starting out say that they sit down to revise but have writer's block. For that, refer to Rivera:

> Embrace your writer's block. It's nature's way of saving trees and your reputation. Listen to it and try to understand its source. Often, writer's block happens to you because somewhere in your work you've lied to yourself and your subconscious won't let you go any further until you've gone back, erased the lie, stated the truth and started over.[3]

Is it really writer's block? Or does the play want to say something that you are too afraid to say? Or is something else going on?

At the end of the metaphorical day, a work of art is never done. All we can do is try our best and release it into the world to find its own life.

Writer Paul Valéry said,

> In the eyes of those who anxiously seek perfection, **a work is never truly completed** – a word that for them has no sense – **but abandoned**; and this abandonment, of the book to the fire or to the public, whether due to weariness or to a need to deliver it for publication, is a sort of accident, comparable to the letting-go of an idea that has become so tiring or annoying that one has lost all interest in it.[4]

Beethoven went through 70 drafts of his symphonies.

Or, as one of my first students put it, "This sh*t is so f**kin' hard!"

Here are five questions to ask yourself during the rewrite process:

(1) Is Someone Actively Pursuing Their Goal?

A character's story should be moving forward, motivated by what they want. Make sure that your conflict is "in the room" – in other words, we should see a character pursuing their goals, their wants. We should see obstacles they face in the path of their goals and see realizations they have about whether or not their goals are worthy to pursue. Often, it's easier to write around a conflict (i.e., hear about things happening when characters are off-stage), but seeing the conflict is much more compelling.

(2) What Will Happen if Your Character Fails/ Succeeds in the Active Pursuit of Their Goal? Have You Created High Stakes for Success or Failure?

Remember that stakes can be physical, emotional, spiritual, and/or intellectual. Whatever the stakes are, if a character truly cares about something and is going after it, then we will be more engaged with their journey. What success or failure means in pursuit of this goal give us stakes, gives us a reason to care, and emotionally connects us with the play in a deeper way – for example, "If she fails to find the magic hat, her father will die."

(3) Do I Show Action and Character Rather Than Just Telling the Audience Everything?

Show rather than tell. Theater is alive, unlike a novel or short story that is confined to the page. Our stories and ideas breathe, grow, and change with our audiences – let them see these breaths, this growth, and these changes. For example, if your play is about a painter who is fed up and thinks Warhol's work is awful and overrated, then what's more dramatically interesting: having the painter discuss Warhol being overrated at a museum OR having the painter slash a Warhol canvas at a museum? Both the discussion and the slashing (with some minor dialogue) express pretty much the same sentiment, but the slashing tells a more dynamic, visual story while adding higher stakes to the situation.

(4) By the End of the Play, Am I Fulfilling a Dramatic Question Posed at the Beginning of the Play?

If the main character's journey could be stated as a question at the beginning of the play based on his want ("Will Joe get the girl or end up alone?" or "Will Sonya become a doctor, or will she drop out of school and devote herself to her music?"), is this question answered by the end of the play?

(5) What Are the Themes/Ideas Behind My Play?

Sometimes the themes/ideas don't emerge until after the first draft or two is written. However, it's always good to think about what the big ideas of the play are and whether or not you're expressing them clearly. Usually the character's need – what they really need to know/learn/see/understand by the end of the play – is linked to the theme/idea of the play. For example, if a character learns to have patience with her younger brother, then the theme is probably connected to an idea like the importance of patience or how patience is a part of familial love.

Pro Tip:

Three Important Things to Remember When Writing a Play With Only Two Characters (also called, a two-hander):

(1) In most successful two-handers, each character has a dramatic arc. This means that each

character has a beginning, middle, and end to their own emotional, intellectual, and/or spiritual journey.

Does this mean that the characters must change? No. Most do, but they do not have to.

What they must do is go on a journey where they gain knowledge and experience. Then they have the opportunity to change at the end of the play – and most choose to change, but sometimes they do not.

For example, in my play *The Arsonists*, the father and daughter both have to decide whether or not to leave their hideout at the end of the play.

The daughter enters the play with the intention of staying in the hideout and continuing her family legacy of arson for profit.

The father enters the play with the intention of leaving the hideout (spoiler alert: he's dead and wants to move on to the other side) without acknowledging the damage that his life's work has done to his daughter and how their shared tradition of arson has contributed to her inability to move on with her life into a productive adulthood.

Throughout the play, the daughter learns about herself and her individual, internal strength. She takes what she's learned and changes her mind – she decides to leave the hideout and leave the family legacy behind, now confident that she can navigate the world on her own.

Throughout the play, the father also learns and grows. While his intention – to leave the hideout and move into the great beyond – remains the same, we see that he has gained knowledge and soothed the pain in his daughter's earthly life, so the leaving is one of peace at the end of the play. Whereas, if he left at the beginning of the play, it would be a leaving of pain and desolation that would have corroded both his life and memories and those of his daughter.

Each character has an arc, one intention changes and the other remains the same, but both have gone on an emotional and intellectual journey with a dramatically satisfying beginning-middle-end structure.

(2) In most successful two-handers, characters are complex and nuanced enough to give us a full picture of their life, even though we do not (usually) see their entire life on-stage. Sometimes this happens through the characters describing their lives, but often, and more effectively on-stage, it happens through their individual actions on-stage and how they react to their thinking/values/ideas being challenged by other characters.

For example, in *The Arsonists*, the differing memories that the father and daughter share about the same difficult event show the different ways that they processed the event. By showing how they viewed the major moments in their lives differently (and how the other responds to the differing view of the events), we see how they were moving through the world and how the outcomes of those major events inform the conflict and decisions they are making on-stage now.

(3) In most successful two-handers, the setting is vitally important. Many folks would say that the setting is always important, and to that I say, "Yes, agreed." However, in a two-character play, the importance of the setting is amplified. This occurs because we only have two characters' perspectives to go on; the physical setting around them becomes more important to the storytelling. The audience is going to draw more conclusions that impact the storytelling from the surroundings, as they have fewer characters from which to draw clues.

For example, in *The Arsonists*, I've set the story in the character's hideout. (The characters are a father-daughter arson team who just experienced a fire-gone-wrong.)

By setting the story in their hideout, I give the audience clues that help them flesh out the characters' world and, hence, their basis for life decisions. From the beginning, the audience knows: (a) these characters are doing something outside the law and need a hideout; (b) these characters are long-time criminals, because their hideout is clearly lived-in; (3) these characters do not make a ton of money from their crimes (the hideout is

> bare) but do it out of passion, making a basic living, and an obligation to a family tradition.
>
> The clues that the hideout set provides the audience allows me to skip a lot of expositional dialogue between the characters, because the audience already has – consciously or unconsciously – absorbed significant information about the characters and their situation. I can proceed with writing an active play, knowing they have much of the basic information that they need to understand my characters' situation simply from the setting of the play.

More Great Revision Questions

Probably the most difficult, and most laborious, part of writing is rewriting. I've already given you questions to ask at the end of your first draft. Here are some more to ask for revisions beyond the first draft:

(1) What are my intentions for what this piece will say, mean, highlight, negate? Am I meeting those intentions in my execution?
(2) What are the physical and emotional journeys of my main character, and are those journeys clear?
(3) What are the physical and emotional journeys of my other characters, and are those journeys clear?
(4) Do I follow the "rules" that I created for my world?
(5) If a character's behavior is inconsistent, do I show the reason for the change or the inconsistency?

(6) Do I use almost every detail of my characters' lives to support the forward motion of the play?

(7) Are there moments when characters are talking about an event where that event can actually be illustrated? Can I turn any moments of chatting into moments of action?

(8) Can I "layer" scenes – i.e., if I have a scene where only one action or revelation happens, can I compress information from multiple scenes to create one longer, more interesting scene?

(9) Do I have any characters that I don't need?

(10) Do I have any scenes that I don't need?

(11) I'm awesome, oh yeah, I wrote a play, go me!

And I'll leave you with some words of wisdom from the Philosopher Aeschylus who said: "From a small seed a mighty trunk may grow."[5]

Notes

1 *A Moveable Feast* by Ernest Hemingway, Scribner; Reprint Edition, 2010
2 *Tips on Revision by* Jessica Huang, Playwrights Center Blog, 2019
3 *36 Assumptions about Playwriting* by José Rivera, 2020, https://howlround.com
4 An essay in the *New French Review* by Paul Valéry, March 1933.
5 "Aeschylus Quotes." *BrainyQuote.com*. BrainyMedia Inc, 2020. September 28, 2020, www.brainyquote.com/quotes/aeschylus_398833

12
The Business of Playwriting

To keep myself sane, and to fend off bitterness, I constantly remind myself that there are two important aspects of my life as a playwright:

(1) The Creative Aspect
(2) The Business Aspect

The Creative Aspect is my favorite, honestly. It's writing and revising plays. It's being in workshops and productions. It's reading and writing and viewing as much as I can, in order to deepen myself as a person and an artist. I am completely in control. It's my space to shape, play, and paint as I choose.

The Business Aspect is awkward and, often, uncomfortable. It encompasses submitting plays, networking at events, and creating marketing materials. It is confronting the reality that producers have to work within a vast matrix of constraints – including budget, location, mission statements, and more – when they select shows for production. And that, no matter how much they love my play, they might not be able to produce it if my play does not fit within their matrix.

I encourage you to keep these two aspects of life as a playwright – the art and the industry – in separate parts of your brain and create your own metrics for success in both areas. That way, I feel, we are less likely to fall into bitterness against other artists and can lead a more fulfilling life in the theater.

A few business tips...

Websites

Your website is your professional front porch. It should be maintained as a professionally updated site at all times.

At the very minimum, your website should include: a professional headshot, a bio, work samples, and contact information.

Remember that when a theater company looks you up, they want to be able to find what they need quickly and easily. Keep it clean and without distractions.

Join the New Play Exchange

The New Play Exchange is an online resource where you can post work, and producers can search for work based on what they are interested in producing. Make sure to fill out the entire form for each play that you post, including keywords and phrases. The search engine uses these keywords and phrases to help match your play to a producer: newplayexchange.org

Keep Learning

You can find many wonderful workshop and class options, both online and in person, for a variety of price points. A few of the organizations that hold classes that my students have found useful are: The Playwrights Center, The Dramatist Guild Institute, The Kennedy Center's Playwrights Intensive, The Kennedy Center American College Theatre Festival (for college students only), The Playwrights Foundation, and Ashland New Play Festival.

Resource Links

Following are programs that allow for open submission and have opportunities for you to both develop work and showcase plays.

Pro Tip:

Most submission deadlines occur around the same time every year, so consider putting a reminder in your calendar the month prior to each deadline that renews each year automatically. That way, you'll be reminded a month in advance each year to check the deadline and opportunity in case you want to apply again.

Applying many times is key. First, most selection committees rotate, so it is a great way to get your work in front of a lot of new eyes at once. Second, it usually takes multiple times applying to be accepted. Infamous examples include Paula Vogel applying for New Dramatists over a dozen times before they accepted her.

- PlayPenn New Play Conference: www.playpenn.org/the-conference/
- The Lark Playwrights Week: www.larktheatre.org/what-we-do/our-initiatives/playwrights-week/
- Seven Devils Playwrights Conference: www.idtheater.org/seven-devils.html
- Bay Area Playwrights Festival: http://playwrightsfoundation.org/
- The Eugene O'Neill Theater Center National Playwright Conference: www.theoneill.org/
- Latinx Carnaval of New Work: http://howlround.com/2018-ltc-carnaval-of-new-latinx-work
- Philly Women's Theatre Fest: http://phillywomenstheatrefest.org/
- Ma-Yi Writers Lab: http://ma-yitheatre.org/about-the-lab/
- New Dramatists Playwright Residency: http://newdramatists.org/
- Playwrights Realm Scratch Pad Series and Writing Fellowships: www.playwrightsrealm.org/
- New Georges JAM and Audrey Residency: www.newgeorges.org/category/projects-events/
- WP Lab: http://wptheater.org/lab/
- National Black Theater Playwrights Residency: www.nationalblacktheatre.org/playwrights-residency
- JAW West Festival: www.pcs.org/jaw (sometimes this is open submission, and sometimes it is agent-only submissions)
- Playwrights Center, Various Programs: https://pwcenter.org/programs/core-writer-program

- New Harmony Project, Various Programs: www.newharmonyproject.org/
- Sewanee Writers Conference: http://sewaneewriters.org/
- Great Plains Theater Conference: www.gptcplays.com/
- Ground Floor at Berkeley Rep Summer Residency Lab: www.berkeleyrep.org/groundfloor/summerresidency.asp
- Orchard Project: https://secure.orchardproject.com/
- SPACE at Ryder Farm: www.spaceonryderfarm.org/

Also the New Play Exchange, where you can share work, catches the attention of producers and developers: https://newplayexchange.org/

Developmental Goals

Most companies use developmental goals when trying to assess who is going to use their resources most wisely. They probably have 20 good projects (or more) for every one opportunity slot. For example, the O'Neill received over 1,500 applications this year alone for their summer development opportunities.

So, they want to select projects that are going to get the most out of their resources as well as projects that are interesting/good/have promise.

In general, the three bits of information that organizations want to see in development goals are:

(1) How, specifically, would you use their unique resources?
(2) Why is this project important to develop now?
(3) How does this project, specifically, meet their mission and speak to their audience?

Sometimes they will ask for developmental goals with a specific focus. For example, they'll ask "How does this project fit our missions?" In those cases, make sure to emphasize and/or fully focus on the relationship between your project and their mission. Follow their lead. Again, it would be a huge waste of their time to ask for developmental goals if they were not actually going to look at them closely. So, make sure you pay attention to how they phrase their question and what, if anything, they emphasize.

Examples of developmental goals that have won awards and such...

For a Two-Year Writers Group and Residency Application

I have chosen my newest completed play XXX to submit, because I think it illustrates the growth of both my craft and art over the past two years, a stronger ability to balance more complex structures and more complicated characters as well as combine entertaining thriller-type elements with engaging questions about social issues (in this case, technology and consent).

I relish developing work in a community. At present, this means sharing bits and pieces with colleagues and friends. XXX would give me the opportunity to find a more consistent means of feedback so that my plays could progress more quickly and efficiently. I prefer the company of playwrights during development, especially during the infancy of a play, because playwrights cherish the ugly baby – the idea, scene fragment, or character description with unfulfilled promise – and understand that it takes time to grow out of its eczema, oversized ears, and sharp elbows.

XXX also excites me because it offers time and space to explore how I approach the creation of new work. I want a place where I can experiment with new forms, methods, and rhythms of writing – and where my emphasis on theatricalizing the female experience is embraced and elevated.

As a mother with two young children, who is privileged enough to have the support of family, I am looking for a place to help create a warm, productive, and generous space where, while always a mom, I can also be seen as an artist and individual. I hope that the XXX is that place.

For a 20-Hour Workshop and Staged Reading Process

My goal is to have a draft ready to submit for production after XXX's development process. This play has two (8-hour) readings scheduled: one this summer in XXX and one early in the fall in XXX (this work has never been seen in your city.). Both readings will focus solely on the text, as there is no time to explore the movement sections of the play. I would love to bring what we learn about the text from those readings into the XXX workshop room. I would use the 20-hour process at XXX to explore the movement sections in order to make sure the idea of the movement in my head actually works on-stage as well as explore alternative movement options. This will ensure that I enrich the characters and give full reign to the complexity of their experiences, both in text and in movement – as the play intends. The movement and the text are inextricably linked in telling this story, and I want to give each enough time to fully bloom in the submission-ready draft.

For a One-Day Staged Reading Process

The draft of XXX that I submitted has not been seen in front of a public audience. Since the play relies heavily on the nuanced comedy of characters lightening the tension, in order to delve into deeper and more sensitive issues surrounding gender inequality, I must get the precarious balance of humor and drama right. At this point, I cannot move forward with revisions until I work with actors and a director to create these delicate moments and then put them on-stage in front of an audience. I need the vital elements of performance and audience reaction to determine the next stage of revision for this piece. In addition, I believe that this play will resonate strongly with your audience, because it fits your theater company's mission of XXXXX by providing a provocative conversation revolving around motherhood, the wage gap, and equal pay.

Artistic Statements

Artistic Statements are much more fluid than Development Goals. Since most organizations cannot afford to fly you in for an interview, the Artistic Statements give the organization a chance to get to know you as a person, your interests, your influences, and your overall dreams.

Some call your artistic statements your "Articles of Artistic Faith." Some call it "Reaching Through the Page to Shake Hands." Some call it "A Hellish Experiment."

No matter how you think of the Artistic Statement, if you are going to apply for productions, grants, etc., then you will probably have to write one.

If an organization asks you to answer specific questions in an Artistic Statement, do it. Again, follow their lead. But usually, Artistic Statements are more about getting to know you. Don't be afraid to color outside the lines a bit and get messy. Some statements are formal; some are casual. Some are written in paragraph form, and some in free verse. What you want to do is bring a sense of yourself, your individuality, and your uniqueness to the table.

Here are three older versions of my artistic statement. They are not my favorite pieces of writing, but they did the trick to win awards and fellowships:

(1)

Stories reflect who we are, where we came from, and where we want to go. They are the moral touchstone for societal wounds; they help us navigate, interpret, and transcend. For me, the visceral interplay between audience and live performance is the source of theater's unique power. To tell a story directly to another person, to connect with one another, and to be understood by one another is a basic human need that playwriting serves in a way that writing to the page alone cannot. In a world increasingly dominated by screens, this experience becomes even more rare and its potential impact more powerful. Live theater provides both distance from and intimacy with these stories. It allows us to see ourselves in a new light and be moved and changed by the experience. By finding the extraordinary in the quotidian, I can explode the rut in which audiences live, overturning assumptions and exposing false paradigms. Once destroyed, we rebuild together. Truth becomes an evolving emotional experience, a journey we are always on. I want to mine a deeper understanding and compassion for the other in the room, which, I hope, audiences take with them into their own rooms.

(2)

I am not a garret playwright. I write in motion. I do most of my writing between bouts of pacing that my kids call "the work walk." I've only been able to sit still in the theater. There is a peace that descends when the lights dim and curtain rises or I crack open a copy of a new play.

I had no idea that I was a playwright. I was 12 years old and writing short stories about places I'd never seen but desperately wanted to go. The descriptive passages in my stories kept shrinking while the dialogue steadily grew until they took over one page and then another and then them all. My eighth grade English teacher handed me a used copy of *The Crucible* and said, "You're a playwright. Don't ever turn in another story again. They are awful." And I didn't. But I read *The Crucible* over and over until the binding wore through and the pages fell out. My first plays were also awful, but playwriting gave me a way to find my place in the world, to understand how I saw things and what I thought about them. My characters gave me access to parts of myself that I never knew existed – and also spoke deeply to the students around me (whom I roped into reading aloud in the cafeteria). It was miraculous and transformative. I went from a quiet, nerdy kid to a loud, nerdy kid. I was sometimes silenced but gained the confidence to know that I had a voice and could use it. There was no theater community in rural North Florida, where I was born and raised. While I regretted that at the time, later I appreciated the opportunity to develop my work and voice free of external restrictions of what was "right" writing and "wrong" writing; instead, the focus was simply on doing, exploring, finding, refining, and sharing.

I spent my twenties and early thirties drifting. From Sarasota to San Diego, everywhere I travelled, I found artists working in a myriad of ways. We wandered around inside each other's imaginations in a school basement in Atlanta, a dilapidated beach house in Sarasota, a deserted dance hall in Lisbon, a warehouse in Los Angeles.

During my travels, I learned that there were conversations being had, ideas being realized, beyond anything I ever imagined back in Florida. I felt challenged. I was determined to push harder, to write better. Readings and workshops led to productions. I saw how my plays connected to a larger community of writers and the broader conversation about what it is to create theater and why we do it. These conversations exhilarated me, and I continue to seek them out.

A room full of writers is still my favorite place to be.

Although I've settled down a bit, living in the New York-New Jersey-Philadelphia corridor, my driving need for active, engaged, challenging conversation and creation has never diminished. I feel that this is the optimal moment for me to enter the Core Writers Program, because I am transitioning into a newer, more sophisticated stage of writing (I hope).

I'm seeking a community that will support my transition and encourage my growth as I take on more emotionally, politically, and structurally complex ideas. My two newest pieces bring a more ambitious, epically theatrical sense to stories that are both emotionally intimate and more directly engage with and comment on social and political realities.

The XXXXX has shaped many of the playwrights that I find the most engaging and inspiring in American theater. I would be honored to work, study, learn, and create with you. I'm hoping that you can help me make this transition to stronger, more vital, and necessary work. In return, in my small way, I hope that I can encourage and support other emerging voices by being a part of your community.

(3)

I write deeply rooted characters with a sense of history, whose urgency is reflected in contemporary issues. My characters have a sense of humor about themselves and the world that opens audiences' hearts to challenging perceived realities of gender, identity, and personhood. I often write about characters who live in the forgotten parts of America – in the cracks and crevices that make our country whole. I believe that play is the door to imagination. Imagination is the door to possibility. And possibility is the door to the soul.

> "The world is violent and mercurial – it will have its way with you. We are saved only by love – love for each other and the love that we pour into the art we feel compelled to share: being a parent; being a writer; being a painter; being a friend. We live in a perpetually burning building, and what we must save from it, all the time, is love."
>
> – Tennessee Williams

Amen!
Like Brother Williams, I write for love.
Physical love.
Emotional love.
Intellectual love.
Terminal love.
Fleeting love.
Love that makes characters break out into song.
Love that makes characters kill.
Love that wills dead characters back to life.

I write to explore and expose the enigma wrapped inside a riddle wrapped inside our desperate and adorable need to love and be loved in return.
(Okay, the last bit is from a David Bowie song . . . but he's not wrong!)
The need to be loved, i.e., to be seen,
As we are
As we could be
To be imagined at our best
And Insta-filtered over at our worst
Is what everyone strives for.
So why pretend it is any different?

Why not use that profound need – rooted in all of us – a shared rooting – a shared starting place?
If we begin, with any character, and figure out who and what and why they love.
Then, we have a set of keys to their inner life.
And once we have the keys,
We can begin to unlock all of their other passions and secrets,

> To find the story that they need to tell most of all.
> And that's the one – the gooey, all too human one, that I want to tell.
> That story connects us to our humanness and to the humanness of the characters on-stage and to the rest of humanity, seen and unseen.
> That connecting builds empathy.
> That empathy creates compassion and vision
> And that vision contains the possibility of change, for good.
> (Okay, I stole that line too, from *Wicked* . . ., but again, not wrong.)

Creating Your Own Metric for Success

I love being a playwright. I also recognize that while I can control much of my own writing, and even develop plays with friends and colleagues, the final step into production is fully out of my hands.

As someone who has worked as a literary manager and dramaturg for numerous theaters, I will guarantee you this: You could write the best play in the world, but it might not get selected for production. Theater companies have to select plays that fit into a complex matrix of needs – cast size, theme, funding opportunities, donor interests, audience interests, and more.

However, I do think that there is a home for every voice. It just might not be the home that you expect. Or you might have to build it yourself with a collection of trusted collaborators.

Performer Audra McDonald said: "All you can do is good work, and do the good work for the sake of doing good work and your evolution as an artist."[1]

Finding a Community for Your Voice

One of the most effective ways to find theaters that are interested in your voice and the type of stories that you want to tell is to look at play publishers' websites. Read the synopses of recently released plays. Find plays that live in the same artistic universe as yours, and then look up the development and production history online (just using the Google Machine). Then check and see if those companies accept open submissions. That way you are submitting to organizations that are interested in the type of work that you create.

If you do decide to produce your own work, that's great! There's a long tradition of playwrights producing their own work. But do make sure to connect with producers and other knowledgeable members of your theater community to discuss the logistics of producing in your specific community. Each community has a different range of free and low-cost resources for artists, and you want to make sure that you take advantage of every resource available to you.

Businessman Wayne Huizenga said: "Some people dream of success, while other people get up every morning and make it happen."[2]

Notes

1 *100 Quotes Every Artist Should Know,* The Producer's Perspective, www.theproducersperspective.com/my_weblog/2019/04/100-quotes-every-theater-producer-playwright-director-actor-etc-must-read.html
2 "Wayne Huizenga Quotes." *BrainyQuote.com.* BrainyMedia Inc, 2020. September. 30, 2020, www.brainyquote.com/quotes/wayne_huizenga_703954

Appendix A
For Further Study

(in alphabetical order by title)

Books for New/Early Career Artists

- *Letters to a Young Artist* by Anna Deavere Smith
- *A Masterclass in Dramatic Writing: Theater, Film, and Television* by Janet Neipris
- *Playwriting Brief & Brilliant* by Julie Jensen (a pocket primer for playwriting)
- *Playwrights on Playwriting* by Toby Cole
- *Playwrights Teach Playwriting 1 & 2* edited by Joan Herrington
- *The Science of Storytelling* by Will Storr
- *There Must Be Happy Endings* by Megan Sandberg-Zakian

Online Tools

- *36 Assumptions About Playwriting* by José Rivera (Google it, it appears on many writing sites)
- *The Bake-Off* by Paula Vogel (from her website)
- *Beth Blickers on Finding an Agent* (from the New Dramatists Podcast, Episode 3)

- Chicago's "Not in Our House" standards of behavior for theater and the rehearsal room (from the Not in Our House website)
- *Confessions of a Sexist Playwright* by Jerrod Bogard (from HowlRound)
- *Danger of a Single Story* by Chimamanda Ngozi Adichie (from TED Talks videos)
- *Guidelines to Critical Response* by Liz Lerman (from her website)
- *How to Make your Space TGNC Safe* by Futaba Shioda (from New Dramatists or Shioda's website)
- *Pixar's 22 Rules of Story* (Google it, it appears on many writing sites)
- *Unpacking the Invisible Knapsack* by Peggy McIntosh (from the Racial Equity Toolkit)
- *Visit to a Small Planet* by Elinor Fuchs (from Project Muse)
- *Who Gets to Write What?* by Kaitlyn Greenidge (from the New York Times)

More Great Theater Books. . .

- *100 Essays I Don't Have Time to Write: On Umbrellas and Sword Fights, Parades and Dogs, Fire Alarms, Children, and Theater* by Sarah Ruhl
- *The Art & Craft of Playwriting* by Jeffrey Hatcher
- *Backwards and Forwards* by David Ball
- *Changed for Good* by Stacy Wolf
- *The Dramatist's Toolkit* by Jeffrey Sweet
- *The Empty Space* by Peter Brook

- *Essential Dramaturgy: The Mindset and Skillset* by Theresa Lang
- *The Great White Way* by Warren Hoffman
- *Hitchcock Truffaut* (technically a film read, but a wonderful series of interviews for learning about visual storytelling)
- *An Ideal Theater* by Todd London
- *Look, I Made a Hat* by Stephen Sondheim
- *Moment Work: Tectonic Theater Project's Process of Devising Theater* by Moises Kaufman and Barbara Pitts McAdams
- *Theater Artists Making Theatre With No Theater* Various Authors
- *Towards a Poor Theatre* by Jerzy Grotowski
- *The Viewpoints Book: A Practical Guide to Viewpoints and Composition* by Anne Bogart

Appendix B
Basic Vocabulary, Formatting, and A Note on the Recommended Reading

Basic Playwriting Vocabulary

Action: Something a character does to get what they want

Acts: An "Act" is simply a unit of storytelling.

Acting Edition: A published playscript that is used in productions, usually after the world premiere

Antagonist: A character impeding the journey of the protagonist

Beat: A deliberate pause for effect or change of intention or tactic. In acting, a "Unit" is a collection of beats that have a sense of completion.

Character: The characters that form a part of the story in the drama. Each character in a play has a personality of its own and has a distinct set of principles and beliefs.

Collaboration: Working together to realize shared goals

Conflict: A struggle between opposing forces in a play. The conflict may occur within a character as well as between characters. If the conflict occurs within a character, then there must be a way to show that conflict externally, on-stage.

Dialogue: Two or more characters speaking with each other

Downstage: The part of the stage closest to the audience

Draft: A version of a play

Dramaturg: A collaborator and fellow artist who offers thoughts, questions, research, and other pertinent support to playwrights

Dramaturgy: The art of the dramaturg which ranges from directly supporting the playwright to creating audience engagement materials to creating research packets and more

Ensemble: Artists working together as a group

Exposition: Exposition is the sharing of salient information/backstory with the audience, where needed, in order to allow the audience to follow the action and know what's at stake. Ideally, exposition is imbedded in the action or tactic of a character. The traditional exposition used at the beginning of the play may set the atmosphere and tone, explain the setting, introduce the characters, and provide the audience with any other information necessary to understand the plot.

Expressionism: A style in which everything is seen through the eyes of the central character, and that gaze is often distorted and fragmented.

Monologue: A story or speech given by a character as part of a scene or alone on-stage. A soliloquy is one form of a monologue. In a soliloquy, a character speaks to themselves out loud.

Naturalism: Also called "slice of life," a style in which everything happens as it would in real life

Place: Location where the play takes place – for example, a middle-school English class

Plot: The sequence of events within the play itself

Point of Attack: The first thing an audience sees or hears at the beginning of the play

Protagonist: A character going after something, usually the main focus of the play

Realism: Also called "objective view," a style in which there is a carefully constructed plot

Scene: A continuous moment where a character or characters are in relationship to one another, usually through conversation

Stage Directions: Instructions in the text of a play which are not spoken

Stage Left: The left side of the stage when you are standing on-stage facing the audience

Stage Right: The right side of the stage when you are standing on-stage facing the audience

Stakes: What happens if a character fails or succeeds. This fuels the audience's connection to the character because, generally, the audience cares whether or not the character fails or succeeds.

Story: The plot as well as everything surrounding the plot, how the characters feel, unexpected happenings, what happened before the play begins, and what happens off-stage

Subtext: The feelings behind the words a character speaks

Surrealism: A style in which unrelated scenes are juxtaposed to create meaning, usually via metaphors

Symbolism: Also called "subjective view," a style in which occurrences are episodic, disjointed, and/or distorted

Time: Time is when the events in the play take place – for example, present day, 2002, 1984, or 3040

Upstage: The side of the stage closest to the back wall

World Premiere: The first full production of a theatrical piece

Writing Partner: Someone you partner with to keep each other accountable for deadlines and/or switch pages with for feedback

Formatting

The format that is used to publish plays is often different from the formatting used when playwrights write the plays. That is because play publishers want to get as many words on a page as possible – if they use less paper, it costs less to publish the script. That's why acting editions are often printed in small print with all of the lines squished together.

Playwrights, themselves, write their drafts in many different ways. So whatever works for you, whatever helps your writing energy flow, use that format. Playwright Paula Vogel talks about having "plasticity on the page," which means giving yourself permission to create the text on the page in any visual way that you want, including adding drawings or other visual images. Whether or not more formal editors will publish plays this way, how the text looks can give your collaborators an insight into how to perform the play.

When it comes time to submit the play for consideration for an opportunity, check in with whomever you are submitting the work to see in what format they prefer to receive submissions, and use that format.

If they simply say "a professional format," then check out The Dramatists Guild website (www.dramatistsguild.com). They usually have information on current professional formatting standards available online.

A Note on the Recommended Readings

All of the plays recommended within this text are published and available for purchase in English. Usually, you can search for them online and find them easily. I did this to facilitate the learning experience and make sure that readers have easily accessible plays, where they can clearly see the craft and art of playwriting in practice. However, there are cultural, political, and economic aspects to which plays are published when and for what reasons; so please be aware that there are many great plays that go unpublished as well and many great plays that are published that I did not have the space to include in this book. Please treat this reading list as a starting point for teaching and conversation, rather than an end-all-be-all list of plays to consume.

Appendix C
Additional Worksheet and Writing Prompts

Full-Length "Well-Made Play" Structure Worksheet

Stages in the Structure of a "Well-Made Play"	How the Plot of a Play Develops	Plot Development in _____ (Title of Your Play)
Preliminary Situation/Status Quo	Establish the world of the characters and the play.	
Inciting Incident	An ACTION that complicates the characters' world and/or compromises the characters.	
Rising Action	The series of events following the initial incident. All, or nearly all, important characters are introduced, and the goals of and obstacles facing the protagonists are revealed.	

Moments of Crisis (Reversals) OR Moments of Complication Usually, these moments become more intense and dramatic as the play moves forward.	The character finds a "solution" to whatever action complicated their world, but it creates a future complication. This occurs several times – where a character "solves" something, but the solution creates larger problems. The character's world unravels.	
Climax	The turning point of the action. Moment when the conflict is resolved – you know who wins.	
Falling Action	An event or series of events following the climax. It is usually much shorter than the rising action.	
Conclusion	The outcome of the preceding action – the success or failure, happiness or sorrow of the characters.	

A Few Extra Writing Prompts
Prompt Inspired by Amadeus *by Peter Schaffer*

(1) Pick a memorable moment in history, one that you wish you had witnessed.
(2) Write a scene based on that moment. It can be during that moment, before, after, or long after, reflecting on something that moment affected.
(3) Re-read the scene. What lesson(s) can that moment, through this scene, teach an audience today? Great "historical" plays are never about history. They are about investigating contemporary issues costumed in the guise of a communal memory.

Prompt Inspired by Art *by Yasmina Reza*

Characters draw different, often conflicting, conclusions when witnessing the same event. The conclusion(s) they draw give us a sense of the lens through which they see the world.

Imagine two different characters watching a kid blow out candles on a birthday cake.

Now, write a scene where two characters converse afterwards: Character 1 saw the kid blow out the candles themself, and Character 2 saw the parent help the kid blow the candles out.

Once done, re-read the scene. What can you learn about that character's morals, values, and worldviews from their understanding of this small active moment? In your plays, how can you turn moments where you intellectualize morals, values, and worldviews into active moments that are more engaging to watch on-stage?

Prompt Inspired by Jitney *by August Wilson*

(1) Pick a location in your neighborhood that you go to often but don't think deeply about (grocery store, taxi stand, etc.).

(2) Think about a type of person that is always there, that you usually take for granted (surly cashier, funny driver, etc.).

(3) Write a monologue from that person's point of view about their everyday life. What does successfully getting through the day mean to them? What is failure? And think about what social, political, and cultural elements inform or shape that metric of failure or success. Often, our most interesting characters are based on compelling people overlooked in everyday life.

Prompt Inspired by M. Butterfly *by David Henry Hwang*

What a character is hiding teaches us as much, if not more, about them than what they share openly.

Pick an object:

Knife
Locket
Tetherball

Manuscript
Cigarette

Pick a character pair:

Parent/Child
Partner/Partner
Boss/Worker
Neighbor/Neighbor
Student/Teacher

Write a scene:

Write a scene between these characters where one person is hiding the selected object from the other, and the one hiding it is caught.

Prompt Inspired by The Mountaintop *by Katori Hall*

Who is someone you've always wanted to have a conversation with – famous or unknown, related or not, living or dead, real or imaginary?

Write the conversation you would have with them.

Look back at the conversation. What does this exercise tell you about what you think is important? Now, consider writing a play around the topic(s).

Prompt Inspired by Top Girls *by Caryl Churchill*

Make a list of political topics that are important to you (for example, desserts).

Select one of those topics.

Now, set a timer for three minutes. Write a fast, short scene or monologue that is related to that topic. Don't think. Just write. Then reset the timer and do this five to eight more times.

Look back at your work. What resonances and characters do you find between these short snippets that could be the foundation for a full play?

Get Inspired With Objects

Create a list of objects – no weapons. The list may include food items, a lighter, a wallet, a cup, a flower, or a doll and larger props, such as a framed picture, a globe, or a computer. Sometimes, it is fun to post on social media that you're looking for interesting props for a writing exercise – again, no weapons – and then use the list of things that friends post.

Now, select a prop from the list.

Select a setting: a kitchen, a classroom, a boardroom, etc.

Write a scene where there are three characters that each feels that the prop is important to them for different reasons.

By the end of the scene, one character gets the prop and exits.

Appendix D
List of Play Recommendations by Chapter

All plays are published in English.

Lists are alphabetical by title.

Chapter 1

- *born bad* by debbie tucker green
- *Cost of Living* by Martyna Majok
- *Death and the King's Horseman* by Wole Soyinka
- *The Glass Menagerie* by Tennessee Williams
- *How I Learned to Drive* by Paula Vogel
- *M. Butterfly* by David Henry Hwang
- *Tribes* by Nina Raine
- *Trouble in Mind* by Alice Childress

NOTE:

> If you are writing short plays, there are numerous "Best of . . ." short play collections published every year. I suggest reading the most recent collections as well as longer plays. These short plays can provide examples of how to create a rich character in a short amount of time.

Some of my favorite published short plays are: *Airborne* by Laura Jacqmin, *Chester, Who Painted the World Purple* by Marco Ramirez, *The Sandalwood Box* by Mac Wellman, *I Dream Before I Take the Stand* by Arlene Hutton, *The Blueberry Hill Accord* by Daryl Watson, *Bake Off* by Sheri Wilner, *On The Porch One Crisp Spring Morning* by Alex Dremann, *The Mercury and the Magic* by Rolin Jones, *Roll Over, Beethoven* by David Ives, *Not a Creature Was Stirring* by Christopher Durang, *Jimmy the Antichrist* by Keith J. Powell, *7 Ways to Say I Love You* by Adam Szymkowicz, *Baggage Claim* by Julia Jordan, and *A Moment Defined* by Cusi Cram.

Chapter 2

- *The Aliens* by Annie Baker
- *Arlington* by Enda Walsh
- *Becky Shaw* by Gina Gionfriddo
- *Bottle Fly* by Jacqueline Goldfinger
- *The Danube* and *Mud* by María Irene Fornés
- *Indecent* by Paula Vogel
- *Hurt Village* by Katori Hall
- *Pass Over* by Antoinette Nwandu
- *Pumpgirl* by Abbie Spallen

Chapter 3

- *Anna in the Tropics* by Nilo Cruz
- *Anowa* by Ama Ata Aidoo
- *Back of the Throat* by Yussef El Guindi

- *The Children's Hour* by Lillian Hellman
- *"Master Harold" . . . and the Boys* by Athol Fugard
- *The Nether* by Jennifer Haley
- *School Girls; or, the African Mean Girls Play* by Jocelyn Bioh
- *Shopping and F*cking* by Mark Ravenhill
- *Top Girls* or *A Number* by Caryl Churchill
- *The Ugly One* by Marius von Mayenburg

Chapter 4

- *Art* by Yasmina Reza
- *Cambodian Rock Band* by Lauren Yee
- *Detroit '67* by Dominique Morisseau
- *Glengarry Glen Ross* by David Mamet
- *Good People* by David Lindsay-Abaire
- *Milk Like Sugar* by Kirsten Greenidge
- *A Raisin in the Sun* by Lorraine Hansberry
- *Shining City* by Connor McPherson
- *The Thanksgiving Play* by Larissa FastHorse

Chapter 5

- *Among the Dead* by Hansol Jung
- *August: Osage County* by Tracy Letts
- *Bengal Tiger at the Baghdad Zoo* by Rajiv Joseph
- *The Crucible* by Arthur Miller
- *Flyin' West* by Pearl Cleage
- *The History Boys* by Alan Bennett
- *Intimate Apparel* or *Sweat* by Lynn Nottage
- *The Lieutenant of Inishmore* by Martin McDonagh

Chapter 6

- *Elliot, A Soldier's Fugue* by Quiara Alegría Hudes
- *For Colored Girls . . .* by Ntozake Shange
- *Funnyhouse of a Negro* by Adrienne Kennedy
- *Let Me Down Easy* by Anna Deavere Smith
- *Mary Stuart* by Jean Stock Goldstone and John Reich
- *Master Class* by Terrence McNally
- *The Piano Lesson* by August Wilson
- *Three Tall Women* by Edward Albee

Chapter 7

- *By the Bog of Cats* by Marina Carr, based on *Medea* mythology
- *Electra/Elektra* by Euripides, translated by Anne Carson
- *Electricidad* by Luis Alfaro, based on *Elektra* by Euripides
- *Eurydice* by Sarah Ruhl, based on *Eurydice* mythology
- *Iphigenia Crash Land Falls on the Neon Shell That Was Once Her Heart (a Rave Fable)* by Caridad Svich, based on *Iphigenia at Aulis* by Euripides
- *The Seven* by Will Power, based on *Seven Against Thebes* by Aeschylus (not published but videos available online)

Chapter 8

- *Ain't No Mo'* by Jordan E. Cooper*
- *Booty Candy* by Robert O'Hara

- *Chekhov Lizardbrain* by Pig Iron Theatre Company
- *The Colored Museum* by George C. Wolfe
- *Futurity* by César Alvarez with The Lisps
- *Revolt. She Said. Revolt Again.* by Alice Birch
- *Shock Treatment* by Karen Finley
- *Snow in Midsummer* by Frances Ya-Chu Cowhig
- *That Pretty Pretty; or, The Rape Play* by Sheila Callaghan
- *Untitled Feminist Show* by Young Jean Lee
- *Water & Power* by Culture Clash
- *The Wild Duck* by Henrik Ibsen

Chapter 9

- *9 Parts of Desire* by Heather Raffo
- *Blasted* by Sarah Kane
- *El Grito del Bronx* by Migdalia Cruz
- *The Elaborate Entrance of Chad Deity* by Kristoffer Diaz
- *Curse of the Starving Class* by Sam Shepard
- *Is God Is* by Aleshea Harris
- *The Language Archive* by Julia Cho
- *Lydia* by Octavio Solis

Chapter 10

Wild Theatrical Rides

- *Angels in America* by Tony Kushner
- *Big Love* by Chuck Mee

- *Blown Youth* by Dipika Guha (theater for young audiences)
- *The Body of an American* by Dan O'Brien
- *Caught* by Christopher Chen
- *Collective Rage: A Play in 5 Betties* by Jen Silverman
- *Dublin by Lamplight* by Michael West
- *Failure: A Love Story* by Phillip Dawkins
- *Fairview* by Jackie Sibblies Drury
- *The Fever* by Wallace Shawn
- *Girl Under Grain* by Karen Hartman
- *Goodnight Desdemona, Good Morning Juliet* by Ann-Marie McDonald
- *In Love and Warcraft* by Madhuri Shekar (stage and virtual editions)
- *Kid Simple* by Jordan Harrison
- *The Realistic Jones* by Will Eno
- *Sagittarius Ponderosa* by MJ Kaufman
- *She Kills Monsters* by Qui Nguyen (stage and virtual editions)
- *The Skin of Our Teeth* by Thornton Wilder
- *Slave Play* by Jeremy O. Harris
- *Suicide Forest* by Haruna Lee
- *Underground Railroad Game* by Jennifer Kidwell and Scott R. Sheppard with Lightening Rod Special
- *Woyzeck* by Georg Buchner

Narrative-Focused Plays

- *2.5 Minute Ride* by Lisa Kron
- *Amadeus* by Peter Shaffer

- *The Amen Corner* by James Baldwin
- *Arcadia* by Tom Stoppard
- *B* by Guillermo Calderón
- *Blood and Gifts* by J.T. Rogers
- *Blood Wedding* by Federico Garcia Lorca
- *Bulrusher* by Eisa Davis
- *Buried Child* by Sam Shepard
- *Crooked Parts* by Azure Osborne-Lee
- *Dutchman* by Amiri Baraka
- *Dr. Faustus* by Christopher Marlowe
- *Eight Gigabytes of Hardcore Pornography* by Declan Greene
- *Enfrascada* by Tanya Saracho
- *The First Deep Breath* by Lee Edward Colston II*
- *Fleabag* by Phoebe Waller-Bridge
- *Fuenteovejuna* by Lope de Vega
- *This Heaven* by Nakkiah Lui
- *Hir* by Taylor Mac
- *Holy Ghosts* by Romulus Linney
- *How We Got On* by Idris Goodwin (theater for young audiences)
- *The House of Desires* by Sor Juana Inés de la Cruz
- *In the Blood* by Suzan-Lori Parks
- *The Invisible Hand* by Ayad Akhtar
- *Last Night and the Night Before* by Donnetta Lavinia Grays*
- *Last Summer at Bluefish Cove* by Jane Chambers
- *Marisol* by José Rivera
- *Mauritius* by Theresa Rebeck
- *Mojo* by Jez Butterworth
- *Moon for the Misbegotten* by Eugene O'Neill

- *'Night Mother* by Marsha Norman
- *Off the Rails* by Randy Reinholz*
- *Oohrah!* by Bekah Brunstetter
- *Proof* by David Auburn
- *The Sisters Rosenweig* by Wendy Wasserstein
- *Skin Tight* by Gary Henderson
- *A Soldier's Play* by Charles Fuller
- *Stick Fly* by Lydia Diamond
- *Nora: A Doll's House* by Stef Smith
- *Teenage Dick* by Mike Lew
- *Trifles* by Susan Glaspell
- *Vincent in Brixton* by Nicholas Wright
- *Waiora* by Hone Kouka
- *The Whale* by Samuel Hunter
- *What the Constitution Means to Me* by Heidi Schreck
- *You Got Older* by Clare Barron

Commentary-Focused Plays

- *America v. 2.1: The Sad Demise & Eventual Extinction of The American Negro* by Stacey Rose*
- *The Cherry Orchard* by Anton Chekhov
- *Dead and Breathing* by Chisa Hutchinson (theater for young audiences)
- *Firebird Tattoo* by Ty Defoe
- *Galileo* by Bertolt Brecht
- *The Garden Party* by Václav Havel
- *God's Country* by Steven Dietz
- *Good Goods* by Christina Anderson
- *Heddatron* by Elizabeth Meriweather

- *The Internationalist* by Anne Washburn
- *La Ruta* by Isaac Gómez*
- *The Laramie Project* by Tectonic Theater Project
- *Machinal* by Sophie Treadwell
- *Mississippi Goddamn* by Jonathan Norton
- *P'yongyang* by In-Sook Chappell
- *Paul* by Howard Brenton
- *The Radicalisation of Bradley Manning* by Tim Price
- *Silent Sky* by Lauren Gunderson
- *Sugar in Our Wounds* by Donja Love
- *Underground* by Lisa B. Thompson
- *Until the Flood* by Dael Orlandersmith

*Awaiting publication

Appendix E
Reading Pairing Recommendations Listed by Subject Matter

There are hundreds of ways that the recommended full-length plays in this book can be selected and organized to teach the craft of playwriting for your unique community. Following are just a few ways that you could organize your syllabus; however, please be aware that these lists are based on my limited experience and often lean into the "elective" style of focusing deeply on one type of play or demographic of playwright.

Each play recommended in this book is only listed once. However, many of these plays have intersectional subjects and can be mixed and matched for future syllabi. On a practical level, I try to only teach a play once at each school where I teach so that students can always take my classes and be exposed to new material.

The lists are alphabetical by play title.

Playwriting I/Introduction to Playwriting

- *Bengal Tiger at the Baghdad Zoo* by Rajiv Joseph
- *Cambodian Rock Band* by Lauren Yee
- *The Crucible* by Arthur Miller
- *Eurydice* by Sarah Ruhl

- *Mojo* by Jez Butterworth
- *The Nether* by Jennifer Haley
- *Revolt. She Said. Revolt Again.* by Alice Birch
- *School Girls; or, the African Mean Girls Play* by Jocelyn Bioh
- *The Thanksgiving Play* by Larissa FastHorse
- *Trouble in Mind* by Alice Childress
- *The Whale* by Samuel Hunter

Playwriting II

- *Art* by Yasmina Reza
- *August: Osage County* by Tracy Letts
- *Bottle Fly* by Jacqueline Goldfinger
- *Cost of Living* by Martyna Majok
- *Curse of the Starving Class* by Sam Shepard
- *The Danube* by María Irene Fornés
- *Good People* by David Lindsay-Abaire
- *The House of Desires* by Sor Juana Inés de la Cruz
- *In the Blood* by Suzan-Lori Parks
- *The Lieutenant of Inishmore* by Martin McDonagh
- *Lydia* by Octavio Solis
- *Milk Like Sugar* by Kirsten Greenidge
- *The Piano Lesson* by August Wilson

Playwriting III

- *Back of the Throat* by Yussef El Guindi
- *Blood Wedding* by Federico Garcia Lorca
- *By the Bog of Cats* by Marina Carr
- *Detroit '67* by Dominique Morisseau

- *The Elaborate Entrance of Chad Deity* by Kristoffer Diaz
- *Glengarry Glen Ross* by David Mamet
- *How I Learned to Drive* by Paula Vogel
- *M. Butterfly* by David Henry Hwang
- *Shopping and F*cking* by Mark Ravenhill
- *Suicide Forest* by Haruna Lee
- *Sweat* by Lynn Nottage
- *Tribes* by Nina Raine

Playwriting IV

- *The Aliens* by Annie Baker
- *Angels in America* by Tony Kushner
- *Blasted* by Sarah Kane
- *Caught* by Christopher Chen
- *The Colored Museum* by George C. Wolfe
- *Dr. Faustus* by Christopher Marlowe
- *Hurt Village* by Katori Hall
- *"Master Harold" . . . and the Boys* by Athol Fugard
- *Slave Play* by Jeremy O' Harris
- *Teenage Dick* by Mike Lew
- *Underground Railroad Game* by Jennifer Kidwell and Scott R. Sheppard with Lightening Rod Special

Playwriting With a Focus on Less Utilized Structures

- *Arcadia* by Tom Stoppard
- *Big Love* by Chuck Mee
- *Chekhov Lizardbrain* by Pig Iron Theatre Company

- *God's Country* by Steven Dietz
- *Heddatron* by Elizabeth Meriweather
- *Indecent* by Paula Vogel
- *Machinal* by Sophie Treadwell
- *Snow in Midsummer* by Frances Ya-Chu Cowhig
- *Untitled Feminist Show* by Young Jean Lee

Playwriting With a Focus on Black Playwrights

- *Ain't No Mo'* by Jordan E. Cooper*
- *born bad* by debbie tucker green
- *Dutchman* by Amiri Baraka
- *Flyin' West* by Pearl Cleage
- *Funnyhouse of a Negro* by Adrienne Kennedy
- *Pass Over* by Antoinette Nwandu
- *A Raisin in the Sun* by Lorraine Hansberry
- *Underground* by Lisa B. Thompson

Playwriting With a Focus on the Family

- *Buried Child* by Sam Shepard
- *The Cherry Orchard* by Anton Chekov
- *Electricidad* by Luis Alfaro
- *The First Deep Breath* by Lee Edward Colston II*
- *Holy Ghosts* by Romulus Linney
- *Is God Is* by Aleshea Harris
- *Last Night and the Night Before* by Donnetta Lavinia Grays*
- *Moon for the Misbegotten* by Eugene O'Neill
- *Oohrah!* by Bekah Brunstetter
- *Proof* by David Auburn

- *The Realistic Joneses* by Will Eno
- *Sagittarius Ponderosa* by MJ Kaufman
- *Stick Fly* by Lydia Diamond
- *Trifles* by Susan Glaspell
- *Waiora* by Hone Kouka

Playwriting With a Focus on Female and Non-Binary Playwrights

- *America v. 2.1: The Sad Demise & Eventual Extinction of The American Negro* by Stacey Rose*
- *Becky Shaw* by Gina Gionfriddo
- *Bulrusher* by Eisa Davis
- *The Children's Hour* by Lillian Hellman
- *For Colored Girls . . .* by Ntozake Shange
- *Electra/Elektra* translated by Anne Carson
- *Enfrascada* by Tanya Saracho
- *Good Goods* by Christina Anderson
- *Goodnight Desdemona, Good Morning Juliet* by Ann-Marie McDonald
- *The Internationalist* by Anne Washburn
- *Intimate Apparel* by Lynn Nottage
- *The Language Archive* by Julia Cho
- *Mauritius* by Theresa Rebeck
- *'Night Mother* by Marsha Norman
- *Pumpgirl* by Abbie Spallen
- *Nora: A Doll's House* by Stef Smith
- *The Sisters Rosenweig* by Wendy Wasserstein
- *Top Girls* by Caryl Churchill
- *That Pretty Pretty; or, The Rape Play* by Sheila Callaghan

Playwriting With a Focus on LGBTQIA+ Playwrights

- *The Amen Corner* by James Baldwin
- *Booty Candy* by Robert O'Hara
- *Collective Rage: A Play in 5 Betties* by Jen Silverman
- *Crooked Parts* by Azure Osborne-Lee
- *Firebird Tattoo* by Ty Defoe
- *Futurity* by César Alvarez with The Lisps
- *The Glass Menagerie* by Tennessee Williams
- *Hir* by Taylor Mac
- *The History Boys* by Alan Bennett
- *Kid Simple* by Jordan Harrison
- *Last Summer at Bluefish Cove* by Jane Chambers
- *Master Class* by Terrence McNally
- *Sugar in Our Wounds* by Donja Love
- *Three Tall Women* by Edward Albee

Playwriting With a Focus on Latinx and Hispanic Playwrights

- *Anna in the Tropics* by Nilo Cruz
- *El Grito del Bronx* by Migdalia Cruz
- *Fuenteovejuna* by Lope de Vega
- *Iphigenia Crash Land Falls on the Neon Shell That Was Once Her Heart (a Rave Fable)* by Caridad Svich
- *Marisol* by José Rivera
- *Mud* by María Irene Fornés
- *Water & Power* by Culture Clash

Playwriting With a Focus on History Plays

- *Amadeus* by Peter Shaffer
- *Death and the King's Horseman* by Wole Soyinka
- *Galileo* by Bertolt Brecht
- *La Ruta* by Isaac Gómez*
- *The Laramie Project* by Tectonic Theater Project
- *Mary Stuart* by Jean Stock Goldstone and John Reich
- *Mississippi Goddamn* by Jonathan Norton
- *Off the Rails* by Randy Reinholz*
- *Paul* by Howard Brenton
- *P'yongyang* by In-Sook Chappell
- *Silent Sky* by Lauren Gunderson
- *Vincent in Brixton* by Nicholas Wright
- *What the Constitution Means to Me* by Heidi Schreck

Playwriting With a Focus on One-Person Shows

- *2.5 Minute Ride* by Lisa Kron
- *9 Parts of Desire* by Heather Raffo
- *The Fever* by Wallace Shawn
- *Fleabag* by Phoebe Waller-Bridge
- *Let Me Down Easy* by Anna Deavere Smith
- *Shock Treatment* by Karen Finley
- *Until the Flood* by Dael Orlandersmith

Playwriting With a Focus on Theater for Families and Young Audiences

- *Blown Youth* by Dipika Guha
- *Dead and Breathing* by Chisa Hutchinson

- *Dublin by Lamplight* by Michael West
- *Failure: A Love Story* by Philip Dawkins
- *How We Got On* by Idris Goodwin
- *In Love and Warcraft* by Madhuri Shekar
- *She Kills Monsters* by Qui Nguyen

Playwriting With a Focus on War and Apocalypse

- *Arlington* by Enda Walsh
- *Blood and Gifts* by J.T. Rogers
- *The Body of an American* by Dan O'Brien
- *Elliott, A Soldier's Fugue* by Quiara Alegría Hudes
- *Girl Under Grain* by Karen Hartman
- *The Invisible Hand* by Ayad Akhtar
- *The Radicalisation of Bradley Manning* by Tim Price
- *The Skin of Our Teeth* by Thornton Wilder
- *A Soldier's Play* by Charles Fuller
- *Woyzeck* by Georg Buchner

Playwriting With a Focus on Writers Outside the United States

- *Among the Dead* by Hansol Young (South Korea)
- *Anowa* by Ama Ata Aidoo (Ghana)
- *B* by Guillermo Calderón (Chile)
- *Eight Gigabytes of Hardcore Pornography* by Declan Greene (Australia)
- *The Garden Party* by Václav Havel (Czech Republic)
- *This Heaven* by Nakkiah Lui (Gamillaroi/Torres Strait Islander, Australia)

- *A Number* by Caryl Churchill (England)
- *Shining City* by Connor McPherson (Ireland)
- *Skin Tight* by Gary Henderson (New Zealand)
- *The Ugly One* by Marius von Mayenburg (Germany)
- *The Wild Duck* by Henrik Ibsen (Norway)

And Here Are a Few of My Personal Favorites to Teach

- *2.5 Minute Ride* by Lisa Kron**
- *Amadeus* by Peter Shaffer**
- *Among the Dead* by Hansol Young
- *Anowa* by Ama Ata Aidoo
- *Arlington* by Enda Walsh**
- *Bengal Tiger at the Baghdad Zoo* by Rajiv Joseph**
- *Cambodian Rock Band* by Lauren Yee**
- *Caught* by Christopher Chen**
- *The Children's Hour* by Lillian Hellman
- *Cost of Living* by Martyna Majok**
- *The Crucible* by Arthur Miller
- *Curse of the Starving Class* and *Buried Child* by Sam Shepard
- *The Danube* and *Mud* by María Irene Fornés
- *Detroit '67* by Dominique Morisseau
- *The Elaborate Entrance of Chad Deity* by Kristoffer Diaz
- *Elliot, A Soldier's Fugue* by Quiara Alegría Hudes**
- *Heddatron* by Elizabeth Meriweather
- *Failure: A Love Story* by Phillip Dawkins
- *Fairview* by Jackie Sibblies Drury
- *The Fever* by Wallace Shawn

- *Girl Under Grain* by Karen Hartman
- *Glengarry Glen Ross* by David Mamet
- *Good Goods* by Christina Anderson
- *The House of Desires* by Sor Juana Inés de la Cruz
- *How I Learned to Drive* by Paula Vogel
- *Hurt Village* by Katori Hall
- *In the Blood* by Suzan-Lori Parks
- *Is God Is* by Aleshea Harris**
- *The Language Archive* by Julia Cho
- *Let Me Down Easy* by Anna Deavere Smith
- *The Lieutenant of Inishmore* by Martin McDonagh**
- *Intimate Apparel* by Lynn Nottage
- *Lydia* by Octavio Solis**
- *La Ruta* by Isaac Gómez*/**
- *Milk Like Sugar* by Kirsten Greenidge
- *The Nether* by Jennifer Haley**
- *A Number* and *Top Girls* by Caryl Churchill
- *Oohrah!* by Bekah Brunstetter
- *Pass Over* by Antoinette Nwandu
- *Paul* by Howard Brenton
- *The Skin of Our Teeth* by Thornton Wilder
- *Stick Fly* by Lydia Diamond
- *The Thanksgiving Play* by Larissa FastHorse**
- *Trouble in Mind* by Alice Childress
- *Underground Railroad Game* by Jennifer Kidwell and Scott R. Sheppard with Lightening Rod Special**
- *The Whale* by Samuel Hunter**
- *What the Constitution Means to Me* by Heidi Schreck

*Awaiting publication

**Student favorites

Appendix F
Reading Recommendations Listed by Publisher

Reading recommendations listed by publisher. Most can be found, or ordered through, all major bookstores online and in person.

A Note About "Collections" for Teachers. . .

When possible, I recommend students purchase a collection of a playwright's work, rather than one script. That way, the students have more resources to easily access. The exception to this rule is translations; I always try to find my idea of the best translation of a text that students will be able to access.

I also attempt to find a trade paperback, rather than an acting edition, of each text when possible. I've found that students new to theater have an easier time reading the trade version of a play.

In addition, for extra credit in my class, you can read one or more of the play(s) in the collections that have not been assigned and write an essay about it/them. This encourages students to "follow their own noses," as my father used to say, or explore on their own, which can boost their confidence and increase their aesthetic vocabulary to help them define their own voice on the page.

The following list is alphabetical by title.

53rd State Press

- *Chekhov Lizardbrain* by Pig Iron Theatre Company
- *Suicide Forest* by Haruna Lee

Australian Plays

- *Eight Gigabytes of Hardcore Pornography* by Declan Greene
- *This Heaven* by Nakkiah Lui

Back Bay Books

- *The Invisible Hand* by Ayad Akhtar

Broadway Licensing/Dramatists Play Service

- *Caught* by Christopher Chen
- *The Children's Hour* by Lillian Hellman
- *Holy Ghosts* by Romulus Linney
- *'Night Mother* by Marsha Norman
- *School Girls; or, the African Mean Girls Play* by Jocelyn Bioh
- *Silent Sky* by Lauren Gunderson
- *Sugar in Our Wounds* by Donja Love

Broadway Play Publishing

- *Iphigenia Crash Land Falls on the Neon Shell That Was Once Her Heart (a Rave Fable)* by Caridad Svich
- *Mississippi Goddamn* by Jonathan Norton

Chuck Mee's Website

- *Big Love* by Chuck Mee

City Lights Publishers

- *Shock Treatment* by Karen Finley

Concord Theatricals/Samuel French

- *Among the Dead* by Hansol Jung
- *Booty Candy* by Robert O'Hara
- *The Elaborate Entrance of Chad Deity* by Kristoffer Diaz
- *Enfrascada* by Tanya Saracho
- *Eurydice* by Sarah Ruhl
- *Funnyhouse of a Negro* by Adrienne Kennedy
- *God's Country* by Steven Dietz
- *In Love and Warcraft* by Madhuri Shekar
- *Lydia* by Octavio Solis
- *Milk Like Sugar* by Kirsten Greenidge
- *Oohrah!* by Bekah Brunstetter
- *She Kills Monsters* by Qui Nguyen
- *A Soldier's Play* by Charles Fuller
- *Stick Fly* by Lydia Diamond
- *Trifles* by Susan Glaspell

Dial Press

- *Buried Child* and *Curse of the Starving Class* by Sam Shepard, in collection *Sam Shepard: Seven Plays*

Dover

- *The Cherry Orchard* by Anton Chekhov
- *Dr. Faustus* by Christopher Marlowe
- *Fuenteovejuna* by Lope de Vega (dual-language edition: Spanish and English)
- *The Wild Duck* by Henrik Ibsen

Faber and Faber

- *Arcadia* by Tom Stoppard, in collection *Tom Stoppard*
- *By the Bog of Cats* by Marina Carr
- *The Fever* by Wallace Shawn, in collection *Wallace Shawn: Plays 1*
- *The History Boys* by Alan Bennett
- *Pumpgirl* by Abbie Spallen

Farrar, Straus and Giroux

- *Art* by Yasmina Reza
- *Blood and Gifts* by J.T. Rogers
- *Electra/Elektra* by Euripides, translated by Anne Carson, in collection *An Oresteia*
- *Proof* by David Auburn

Grove Press

- *The Colored Museum* by George C. Wolfe
- *The Garden Party* by Václav Havel, in collection *The Garden Party and Other Plays*

- *Glengarry Glen Ross* by David Mamet
- *Goodnight Desdemona, Good Morning Juliet* by Ann-Marie McDonald
- *Pass Over* by Antoinette Nwandu

Harper Perennial

- *Amadeus* by Peter Shaffer
- *The Skin of Our Teeth* by Thornton Wilder
- *Dutchman* by Amiri Baraka, in collection *Two Plays by LeRoi Jones*

Huia Bookshop

- *Waiora* by Hone Kouka

JH Press

- *Last Summer at Bluefish Cove* by Jane Chambers

Literary Licensing

- *Mary Stuart* by Jean Stock Goldstone and John Reich

Mariner Books

- *The Sisters Rosenweig* by Wendy Wasserstein

Methuen Drama

- *Anowa* by Ama Ata Aidoo, in collection *Contemporary African Plays*

- *Back of the Throat* by Yussef El Guindi, in collection *The Selected Work of Yussef El Guindi*
- *Becky Shaw* by Gina Gionfriddo
- *Blasted* by Sarah Kane, in collection *Sarah Kane: Complete Plays*
- *Blood Wedding* by Federico Garcia Lorca (student edition)
- *Bulrusher* by Eisa Davis, in collection *The Methuen Drama Book of Post-Black Plays*
- *Crooked Parts* by Azure Osborne-Lee, in collection *The Methuen Drama Book of Trans Plays*
- *Death and the King's Horseman* by Wole Soyinka, in collection *Contemporary African Plays*
- *Dublin by Lamplight* by Michael West
- *Electricidad* by Luis Alfaro, in collection *The Greek Trilogy of Luis Alfaro*
- *Firebird Tattoo* by Ty Defoe, in collection *The Methuen Drama Book of Trans Plays*
- *Good Goods* by Christina Anderson, in collection *The Methuen Drama Book of Post-Black Plays*
- *Hurt Village* by Katori Hall, in collection *Katori Hall Plays: 1*
- *The Lieutenant of Inishmore* by Martin McDonagh (student edition)
- *The Life of Galileo* by Bertolt Brecht (student edition)
- *The Radicalisation of Bradley Manning* by Tim Price
- *Sagittarius Ponderosa* by MJ Kaufman, in collection *The Methuen Drama Book of Trans Plays*
- *Shopping and F*cking* by Mark Ravenhill, in collection *Mark Ravenhill Plays: 1*

- *Skin Tight* by Gary Henderson
- *Snow in Midsummer* by Frances Ya-Chu Cowhig
- *Top Girls* by Caryl Churchill (student edition)
- *The Ugly One* by Marius von Mayenburg

Nick Hern Books

- *Arlington* by Enda Walsh
- *born bad* by debbie tucker green, in collection *debbie tucker green plays: one*
- *Fleabag* by Phoebe Waller-Bridge
- *Machinal* by Sophie Treadwell
- *Nora: A Doll's House* by Stef Smith
- *A Number* by Caryl Churchill, in collection *Caryl Churchill Plays: 4*
- *Paul* by Howard Brenton
- *Shining City* by Connor McPherson
- *Teenage Dick* by Mike Lew
- *Tribes* by Nina Raine
- *Vincent in Brixton* by Nicholas Wright

No Passport Press

- *Girl Under Grain* by Karen Hartman
- *El Grito del Bronx* by Migdalia Cruz, in collection *El Grito del Bronx and Other Plays*

Northwestern University Press

- *9 Parts of Desire* by Heather Raffo
- *The Nether* by Jennifer Haley

- *Trouble in Mind* by Alice Childress, in collection *Selected Plays by Alice Childress*
- *You Got Older* by Clare Barron
- *Underground* by Lisa B. Thompson, in collection *Three Plays*

Oberon Books

- *B* by Guillermo Calderón
- *The Body of an American* by Dan O'Brien, in collection *Dan O'Brien: Plays One*
- *Collective Rage: A Play in 5 Betties* by Jen Silverman
- *The House of Desires* by Sor Juana Inés de la Cruz
- *P'yongyang* by In-Sook Chappell

Oxford University Press

- *Woyzeck* by Georg Buchner

PAJ Publications

- *The Danube* and *Mud* by María Irene Fornés, in collection *María Irene Fornés Plays*

Penguin

- *The Crucible* by Arthur Miller
- *The Glass Menagerie* by Tennessee Williams

Playscripts

- *Blown Youth* by Dipika Guha

- *Dead and Breathing* by Chisa Hutchinson
- *Failure: A Love Story* by Phillip Dawkins
- *Heddatron* by Elizabeth Meriweather
- *Hir* by Taylor Mac, in collection *The Downtown Anthology: 6 Hit Plays from New York's Downtown Theaters*
- *How We Got On* by Idris Goodwin
- *The Internationalist* by Anne Washburn
- *Kid Simple* by Jordan Harrison
- Short plays: *Airborne* by Laura Jacqmin, *Chester, Who Painted the World Purple* by Marco Ramirez, *The Sandalwood Box* by Mac Wellman, *I Dream Before I Take the Stand* by Arlene Hutton, *The Blueberry Hill Accord* by Daryl Watson, *Bake Off* by Sheri Wilner, *On The Porch One Crisp Spring Morning* by Alex Dremann, *The Mercury and the Magic* by Rolin Jones, *Roll Over, Beethoven* by David Ives, *Not a Creature Was Stirring* by Christopher Durang, *Jimmy the Antichrist* by Keith J. Powell, *7 Ways to Say I Love You* by Adam Szymkowicz, *Baggage Claim* by Julia Jordan, and *A Moment Defined* by Cusi Cram

Plume

- *M. Butterfly* by David Henry Hwang
- *Master Class* by Terrence McNally
- *The Piano Lesson* by August Wilson
- *Three Tall Women* by Edward Albee

Scribner

- *For Colored Girls . . .* by Ntozake Shange

Smith & Kraus

- *Mauritius* by Theresa Rebeck, in collection *Theresa Rebeck: Complete Plays Volume IV, 2007–2012*
- *Underground Railroad Game* by Jennifer Kidwell and Scott R. Sheppard with Lightening Rod Special

Soft Skull Press

- *Bengal Tiger at the Baghdad Zoo* by Rajiv Joseph
- *That Pretty Pretty; or, The Rape Play* by Sheila Callaghan, in collection *Three Plays*

Soho Rep Bookshop

- *Futurity* by César Alvarez with The Lisps
- *Is God Is* by Aleshea Harris
- *Revolt. She Said. Revolt Again.* by Alice Birch

Theatre Communications Group (TCG)

- *2.5 Minute Ride* by Lisa Kron
- *The Aliens* by Annie Baker, in the collection *The Vermont Plays: Four Plays*
- *Angels in America* by Tony Kushner
- *Anna in the Tropics* by Nilo Cruz

- *August: Osage County* by Tracy Letts
- *Cambodian Rock Band* by Lauren Yee
- *Cost of Living* by Martyna Majok
- *Detroit '67* by Dominique Morisseau, in collection *The Detroit Project: Three Plays*
- *Elliot, A Soldier's Fugue* by Quiara Alegría Hudes
- *Fairview* by Jackie Sibblies Drury
- *Flyin' West* by Pearl Cleage
- *Good People* by David Lindsay-Abaire
- *How I Learned to Drive* by Paula Vogel
- *In the Blood* by Suzan-Lori Parks, in collection *The Red Letter Plays*
- *Indecent* by Paula Vogel
- *Intimate Apparel* by Lynn Nottage
- *The Language Archive* by Julia Cho, in collection *The Language Archive and Other Plays*
- *Let Me Down Easy* by Anna Deavere Smith
- *Marisol* by José Rivera, in collection *Marisol and Other Plays*
- *Mojo* by Jez Butterworth, in collection *Mojo and Other Plays*
- *The Realistic Jones* by Will Eno
- *Slave Play* by Jeremy O. Harris
- *Sweat* by Lynn Nottage
- *The Thanksgiving Play* by Larissa FastHorse
- *Until the Flood* by Dael Orlandersmith
- *Untitled Feminist Show* by Young Jean Lee
- *Water & Power* by Culture Clash, in the collection *Oh Wild West! The California Plays*
- *The Whale* by Samuel Hunter
- *What the Constitution Means to Me* by Heidi Schreck

Vintage

- *The Amen Corner* by James Baldwin
- *The Laramie Project* by Tectonic Theater Project
- *"Master Harold" . . . and the Boys* by Athol Fugard
- *A Raisin in the Sun* by Lorraine Hansberry

Yale University Press

- *Bottle Fly* by Jacqueline Goldfinger
- *Moon for the Misbegotten* by Eugene O'Neill

Awaiting Publication

(My guess is that these publications have been delayed due to COVID-19.)

- *Ain't No Mo'* by Jordan E. Cooper
- *America v. 2.1: The Sad Demise & Eventual Extinction of The American Negro* by Stacey Rose
- *The First Deep Breath* by Lee Edward Colston II
- *Last Night and the Night Before* by Donnetta Lavinia Grays
- *Off the Rails* by Randy Reinholz
- *La Ruta* by Isaac Gómez

Appendix G
Post-COVID-19 Online Theater

I am incredibly excited to live in a world where theater thrives both online and in person. I know that many of my colleagues are terrified that audience members will substitute the online experience for the in-person experience and not come back to the physical theater space.

While I understand their fear, I think it is misplaced.

We already have many manifestations of live performing arts being shared online – cast albums for musicals, videos of performance art, and more. In addition, we have learned from film and the popular "Extended Versions," "Overlapping Interviews," and other options available online that audiences crave a deeper connection with artistic work, and these online outlets feed that creative hunger while keeping them coming back for more.

I believe that theater as a whole community benefits from online work, by getting more people to engage with live performance and excited to see it in person for themselves.

While programs like The Met Live at the AMC and the National Theater's NT@Home series have been trailblazers in streaming theatrical content filmed live on-stage, COVID-19 has proven to us that there are even more ways to connect broader audiences with theatrical content online.

The following are a few things to think about when creating new theatrical pieces specifically for an online environment:

- **Are you livestreaming or pre-filmed streaming?** Think through the pros and cons of livestreaming versus pre-filmed streaming. While livestreaming provides spontaneity and ability to interact in real time with your audience, pre-filmed streaming usually provides a smoother viewing experience. What type of experience most supports the story, or experience, that you are sharing with your audience? For example, I wrote a Zoom play that required audience participants to choose their own story line, and then they were whisked into a special Break Out room at a specific point in the show. So, we did the play live every night. However, many theaters filmed and posted shows online for a specific amount of time (for a short "run") during COVID-19. These stories did not benefit from audience interaction, so it made sense to provide an experience that was less likely to suffer from technical issues. When deciding when to livestream or pre-film stream, or a mix of both, think both about your technical abilities and resources as well as about which type of streaming will most support the story you are telling/experience you are sharing.

- **What are the strengths and weaknesses of the platform that you are using?** Platforms offer different online sharing features. Explore different platforms before selecting one. When you are exploring platform options, ask yourself: Does this platform highlight the strengths of the piece – for example, if it is a movement piece, will the platform be able to capture and share the movement smoothly in real time? What are the weaknesses of this platform and how will that impact my show? Will this platform integrate with other online resources which I may employ, like Facebook Streaming or Twitter Engagement? Make sure to review the strengths and weaknesses of each platform with your collaborators so that you all understand how you will use the strengths and negate the weaknesses of the platform.
- **Structure?** The Western beginning-middle-end/well-made structure that works online remains the same. However, watching screens can wear out an audience's eyes, and patience, more quickly than watching a live stage production. So, often, more traditional storytelling works are limited to an hour or less and use a miniaturized version of the well-made play structure.
- **What is the future of online production?** I don't know. And I love that I don't know. Not knowing can be frightening, but it also leaves space for the possibility of greatness. If you have an idea for an online project, go for it! We need artistic trailblazers who are willing to pioneer the next great wave of innovation in theater.

I leave you with these final thoughts:

BE BOLD.
BE FEARLESS.
CHARGE YOUR COMPUTER BATTERY.

Index

Page numbers in *italics* indicate a figure on the corresponding page.

3D, writing in 73

act breaks: acts and 50–51; intermissions and 51
acting edition 117
action 8, 43, 117
acts 50–51, 117
Aeschylus 96
Aliens, The (Baker) 21
Amadeus (Schaffer) 124
Anatomy of a Suicide (Birch) 21
Angels in America (Kushner) 8–9
antagonist 34, 117
Archer, William 34
Aristotle 3, 64–67
Arsonists, The (Goldfinger) 92–94
Art (Reza) 124
artistic statements 105–112
audience *see* readers
avant-garde work 69

Baker, Annie 21
Baker, George Pierce 34
beat 117
beginning-middle-end/well-made structure 35–36, 161
Birch, Alice 21
Bottle Fly (Goldfinger) 21
Brook, Peter 41
business, of playwriting 97–113; artistic statements 105–112; keep learning 99; New Play Exchange 98; resource links 99–101; using developmental goals 101–104; websites 98

Campbell, Joseph 58
career artists, books for 114
Chappell, In-Sook 6–7
Character Creation 3
characterization 44
characters 117; action on-stage 8; and audience 30; and conflict 42; creating compelling 1–14; creating profile 47–48; discovering object to 61–62; as element of tragedy 65; and ethics 13; exploring 11; intention question of 43; learning about 4; making choices 9–10; and playwrights 16–17; published plays to study 13; and theme 27, 46; writing dialogue for 7
Chekov, Anton 8
chronological structure 69
Churchill, Caryl 21, 126
collaboration 117
commentary-focused plays 85–86
communal stakes 40
community, finding for voice 112

compelling characters, creating 1–14
conflict 40, 42, 49, 117

Debussy, Claude 70
Detroit '67 (Morisseau) 9
developmental goals: examples of 102–104; use of 101–104
dialogue 15–16, 117; electric 15; as objectives 15; published plays to study 13, 24–25; realistic 18; styles of 18
diction 65
director and actors 20–21, 23
downstage 118
draft 118
dramatic question 40, 91
Dramatic Technique (Baker) 34
Dramatists Guild website 121
dramaturg 118
dramaturgy 118
Dr. Faustus (Marlowe) 77

electric dialogue 15
Elliot, A Soldier's Fugue (Hudes) 9
ensemble 118
environment 30
episodic structure 69
experimental and avant-garde work 69
exploratory monologues 61
exposition 39, 118
expressionism 118

feedback, navigating 74–76
formatting 120–121
Fornés, María Irene 68
Freytag, Gustav 34

genre 29–30
Gideon's Knot (Adams) 9

goals 42–43
Guidelines to Critical Response (Lerman) 75

Hagen, Uta 12
Hall, Katori 126
Heddatron (Meriweather) 77
Hemingway, Ernest 87
Huang, Jessica 87
Huizenga, Wayne 112
Hwang, David Henry 125

idea, theme and 26–27, 38, 46, 91
Ikeda, Daisaku 78
intermission 51

Jackson, Samuel L. 3
Jitney (Wilson) 125
José, F. Sionil 78

Laramie Project, The (Tectonic Theater Project) 77
Law & Order 2
Lerman, Liz 75
likability 40
Limitless Room, theater as 77–86
Linney, Romulus 74
livestreaming 160
live theater 106
Lori-Parks, Suzan 21, 57
Love and Information (Churchill) 21

M. Butterfly (Hwang) 125
McDonald, Audra 112
Miranda, Lin-Manuel 76
monologue 7, 48, 118; exercises 58–60; exploratory 61; published plays 63; short 10–11; structure 57–63

Morisseau, Dominique 77
Mountaintop, The (Hall) 126

narrative-focused plays 83–84
naturalism 118
New Play Exchange 98, 101

objective 43
obstacles 43
online: production, future of 161; tools 114–115
on-stage action, examples of 8–9

performative writing *see* playwriting
personal stakes 40–41
Pinter, Harold 3
place 118
platform, strengths/weaknesses of 161
Play-Making (Archer) 34
plays 35; act breaks and intermissions 51; actions and 9; commentary-focused 85–86; conflicts and questions 40; exposition in 39; giving feedback on 74; idea of 26, 35; list of recommendations 128–136; monologues within 57; narrative-focused 83–85; raising the stakes of 9; short 1, 13, 38–39, 47–50, 52; well-made 34–53; writing (performative) 1, 3, 6, 8, 13, 16–17, 20, 35, 73; writing own 70–71; *see also* business, of playwriting; "well-made play"; writing
playwriting: art/industry 98; basic vocabulary 117–120; business aspect 97; creative aspect 97; as performative writing 8; reading recommendations 137–158; *see also* business, of playwriting; play(s)
plot 26, 65, 119
Poetics (Aristotle) 64–67
point of attack 119
post-COVID-19 online theater 159–162
pre-filmed streaming 160
primary moments exercise 80–81
protagonist 34, 119
punctuation choreography 21

Radner, Gilda 81
readers 8, 30, 73, 106
reading recommendations 137–158
realism 119
recommended readings, note on 121
revision: process 87–96; questions 89–91, 95–96
Reza, Yasmina 4, 124
ritual and pattern structure 69
Rivera, José 68
Romeo and Juliet (Shakespeare) 40
Ruhl, Sarah 78

scene 11, 30, 54–56, 119
Schaffer, Peter 124
Science of Storytelling, The (Storr) 2
Scribe, Eugene 34
serial structure 69
Shange, Ntozake 68

She Kills Monsters (Nguyen) 77
short plays 38–39; exercise 47–50, 52; writing 1, 13
silent moments and stage directions 20–22, 24–25
Slave Play (Harris) 77
sloutline, for short play 52
song 65
Sorkin, Aaron 22
spectacle 65
stage: directions 119; directors 21; left 119; right 119; space 41
stakes 9–10, 23, 40–41, 90, 119
Stanislavski, Konstantin 22
status quo 35
Storr, Will 2
story 26, 119
storytelling rules 36–38
Story Web 79–80
structure 69; beginning-middle-end/well-made structure 35–36, 161; graphic representation of 37; monologue 57–63; scene 54–56; of "well-made play" 36–38;
subtext 22–23, 119
super-objective 43
surrealism 119
symbolism 119

tactics 43–44
talent 12–13
ten-minute play 49
theater books 115–116
theme and idea 26–27, 38, 46, 91
thought 65
time 120

Topdog/Underdog (Lori-Parks) 21
Top Girls (Churchill) 126
tragedy, six elements of 65
Twain, Mark 31–32
two-handers 91–92

upstage 120

Valéry, Paul 89
visual moments 73–74
Vogel, Paula 58, 120

websites 98
"well-made play" 34–53; beginning-middle-end structure 35–36, 161; characterization 44; conflict 42; dramatic question 40; exposition 39; full-length structure worksheet 122–123; goals/obstacles/action/objective 42–43; graphic representation of structure 37; likability 40; published plays to study 53; scene structure for 54; short and one-act 38–39; short play exercise 47–50; stakes 40–41; structure 36–38; tactics 43–44; *see also* beginning-middle-end/well-made structure
"Why Now?" question 12
wild theatrical rides 82–83
Williams, Tennessee 60–61, 109
Wilson, August 19, 57, 125
Woman Laughing Alone with Salad (Callaghan) 77

world premiere 120
writing: character 6; draft 87–88; electric dialogue and silent moments 15–25; monologue 7; partner 120; performative 1, 3, 6, 8, 13, 16–17, 35, 73; prompts 124–127; subtext 22; from theme 27; in 3D 73; well-made ten-minute play 47–50; what you know 31–32